Understanding Japanese Management Practices

Understanding Japanese Management Practices

Parissa Haghirian

Understanding Japanese Management Practices

Copyright © Business Expert Press, LLC, 2010.

First published in 2010 by
Business Expert Press, LLC
222 East 46th Street, New York, NY 10017
www.businessexpertpress.com

ISBN-13: 978-1-60649-118-8 (paperback)
ISBN-10: 1-60649-118-0 (paperback)

ISBN-13: 978-1-60649-119-5 (e-book)
ISBN-10: 1-60649-119-9 (e-book)

DOI 10.4128/9781606491195

A publication in the Business Expert Press International Business collection

Collection ISSN: 1948-2752 (print)
Collection ISSN: 1948-2760 (electronic)

Cover design by Jonathan Pennell
Interior design by Scribe Inc.

First edition: August 2010

10 9 8 7 6 5 4 3 2 1

Printed in Taiwan

Abstract

Today, Japan is the most influential economy in Asia and the second largest economy in the world. Japanese consumers are among the richest in the world, and the Japanese market still provides profitable investment opportunities. Not only are the Japanese able to adopt Western ideas and techniques without problems but they also maintain a very unique perspective of the world.

Japanese management practices are no exception. And this outstanding new book, *Understanding Japanese Management Practices*, gives you and other international managers an in-depth look at Japanese management practices and how these can be implemented into Western corporations. It examines the cultural foundations of Japanese management and explains the most famous Japanese business concepts, such as kaizen, just-in-time, and lifetime employment. It then provides practical advice on how to successfully enter and position Western products in the Japanese market. Finally, it provides an advice on how to negotiate successfully with Japanese business partners and reveals what Western managers can learn from Japanese management practices.

Japanese management practices have had an enormous influence on Western management practices over the past few decades. Many Japanese management practices have become a standard in Western firms. This book will undoubtedly guide you through Japanese business practices and how these practices help to improve business processes and to increase quality and efficiency in numerous corporations worldwide. It will also help you learn more about what Japanese management is and how do Japan's management practices differ from those in the West.

Keywords

Japan, Japanese management, Asia, international management and marketing, culture, cross-cultural management, market entry, negotiations

Contents

Tables

Preface

When I first went to Japan almost 20 years ago, I was a student of international business. To support my expensive language classes in Tokyo, I got a job in a Tokyo firm, where I stayed for more than 2 years. This was my first job, and at that time, I had no comparison with what it would be like to work in a Western firm.

I loved working in a Japanese firm. People were very friendly and supportive, the enthusiasm of employees for their job and their company was enormously high, and there was real team spirit. Even after returning to my home country, I continued to work in a Japanese corporation in Vienna, where I worked at one of Japan's major broadcasting corporations. Work was very demanding, but again, the Japanese team was highly motivated, the atmosphere was family-like, and all employees were treated with great respect.

It was only at the age of 27 that I first entered a Western firm. This was the biggest culture shock I have encountered so far. After being socialized into a Japanese firm for more than 7 years, the Western firm seemed an aggressive and very uncooperative place. I still remember how shocked I was to see great competitiveness between employees—something I had never experienced before. Communication styles were very different as well: In Western firms, employees seemed to be very careful about what they said to each other, whereas in Japan, we had no real secrets within the firm. It took me a few months to recognize the benefits of a Western workplace in which praise is more individually awarded and I was seen more as an individual than as a team member.

I enjoyed working in both systems. But I was always, and still am, amazed how complementary and at the same time how successful both are. Western business practices focus on individuals and gain competitive advantages by using their different views, opinions, and ideas as a larger pool from which to extract ideas that benefit the firm. Japanese organizations stress group orientation and build their competitive advantages on merging each group member's views and attitudes into a larger, new idea.

Western organizations have a stronger focus on differentiating themselves from other firms, whereas Japanese firms do not mind reviving ideas that have been successful in another part of the world.

Both the Western and the Japanese management systems have their strengths and weaknesses, but they both represent very unique ways of looking at the world and at business. No wonder that managers in the East and West develop very different solutions to similar problems. Japanese business practices are not applicable in all Western business challenges, but they often provide solutions that are very different from those found in Western firms. But the differences between management in the East and West often lead to confusion and misunderstandings on both sides. In my classes, students often ask which management style is better, and my answer is always the same: There is no perfect management system. Both the Western and Japanese systems have their flaws and their strong points. Depending on the economic situation, they either lead to success or can lead to failure.

When I set out to become a researcher an international management, my main goal was to investigate and communicate various ways of managing a firm successfully. *Understanding Japanese Management Practices* presents the results of my experience in Japanese firms and my research on the topic. Today, after working most of my professional career in Japanese organizations, I still consider Japanese management practices as very unique and complimentary to Western management practices. These practices can provide a lot of inspiration to managers and researchers outside of Japan and support the development of new solutions to global management challenges. International managers should therefore be familiar with both systems in order to develop a strong and diverse management skill set.

Understanding Japanese Management Practices describes Japan as a place for business and discusses the management practices that made Japan famous throughout the business world. It explains the social concepts on which Japanese management is based and its most famous business practices. The book covers the major management practices known in the West and also presents Japanese techniques and facts that so far have not been discussed in Western media or research. It describes work life in the Japanese firm and shows what non-Japanese managers need to know when doing business with the Japanese. Negotiations with the Japanese and entry into the Japanese market are both discussed, and Japanese business etiquette is explained. The book closes with a chapter on what Western managers can learn from Japanese management practices.

Understanding Japanese Management Practices targets managers, students of business, and students of Japanese anthropology who are interested in modern Japanese management and how Japan's management practices can be used to increase competitive advantage.

Parissa Haghirian
Sophia University
Tokyo, Japan
April 2010

PART I

Characteristics of the Japanese Corporation

CHAPTER 1

Kaizen and Total Quality Management

Japanese companies are known for their customer orientation and their high-quality products. Efficient business processes therefore play a major role in Japanese management, and many Japanese management concepts have been adopted and successfully integrated into Western management techniques and businesses. The most famous concept in a Japanese firm is *kaizen*, or continuous improvement, which is often considered a philosophy and aims at improving and perfecting all management processes within a firm. Another concept, which has become successful in Western firms, is the 5S System, which helps organize business and production processes within the firm.

The high quality with which Japanese products are produced and with which services are performed are based on business practices that are recognized outside of Japan. In this arena, the Japanese have developed and implemented very effective tools for sustaining their competitive quality advantage. In this chapter, you will learn about the most prominent management practices in Japan. Upon completion of this chapter, you will

- know what kaizen is and how it can improve all business processes;
- learn what the 5S System is and how it works;
- learn about the instruments that are used to manage and sustain quality in Japan.

Kaizen

Continuous Improvement

In the West, kaizen is the most well-known concept of Japanese management. Kaizen is the Japanese term for "continuous improvement." Kaizen is neither a single management activity nor a management technique, but it can be best described as a positive attitude or a philosophy of creating the highest value and quality for the customer. The main aspect of kaizen is that it is not about radical and ad-hoc change or turnaround but that it is performed by making small changes on an everyday basis to improve productivity, safety for all employees, and business process effectiveness while reducing waste. The overall goal is to enhance the quality of products and to maximize cost efficiency and the safety of manufacturing processes. The concept is based on two principles. First, kaizen is not restricted to a single management discipline but is considered a part of every single business process. Second, kaizen is a continuous process that is supported by all members of a Japanese organization. Kaizen can therefore be applied to every management process or operation and in every organization. Every process can be improved and should be continuously improved.

The philosophy of kaizen was popularized in the West by Masaaki Imai in his book about kaizen, which created a worldwide interest in the concept. The term itself is not clearly defined and is often confused with concepts like the kanban system, total quality management, and just-in-time management.

Small Changes in Every Process

The Japanese concepts of change and improvement differ from Western ideas on these topics. In a Western firm, change typically refers to "radical" change. If a business process or a strategy is changed, we prefer to see a real difference compared to the original situation. A company turnaround or an entirely new strategy are considered significant changes. Small changes, such as moving a desk from one part of the room to another to improve communication between employees, or other similar activities, are not considered very influential on overall corporate success.

The Japanese have a different attitude toward change. Their ideas of change and improvement are ubiquitous. Every process and activity can be improved at any time. Even small changes, such as moving a desk, are considered important because the changes will improve the situation in the long run. Since Japan is a group-oriented society, any change, adaptation, or improvement must be discussed with a large number of people. Important decisions can never be made by just one person. However, group discussions often do not lead to radical ideas, as too many people are involved and too many viewpoints must be considered—the more people involved, the more mass oriented the decision becomes. Radical changes such as drastic downsizing or adopting a strategy are very difficult to implement in a Japanese firm. Radical decisions are therefore very rare, and improvements in the Japanese workplace are often very subtle and would not be considered very significant from a Western perspective.

Gemba Kaizen and Teian Kaizen

We can distinguish between two types of kaizen: *gemba* (actual workplace) *kaizen* and *teian* (plan) *kaizen*. Gemba and teian kaizen both aim to develop higher production and quality standards. Gemba kaizen is an action-oriented approach and refers to improvement activities that are performed in the actual workplace, such as on the shop floor or on the manufacturing line. Gemba kaizen involves every aspect of everyday work that can be improved. The focus of gemba kaizen lies in small changes that will modify the overall success of the company—not necessarily right away but over time.

Gemba kaizen methods are quality circles and suggestion systems. In quality circles, a specialized team develops and designs ideas concerning how to improve the company's performance. Suggestion systems encourage employees to submit suggestions for improving work processes and customer satisfaction.

Teian kaizen, on the other hand, represents a theory-based approach and refers to strategic improvements that are influenced by top management. Here, the implementation of new processes and practices play the most dominant role. The overall goals of teian kaizen are improved business and manufacturing practices. The most prominent teian kaizen methods include total quality control and just-in-time management.[1]

Kaizen Can Be Applied Anytime and Everywhere

The first step to a kaizen-oriented enterprise is a corporate culture that motivates employees and rewards them for improving work and business processes. Kaizen is a process-oriented approach rather than a result-oriented one. Kaizen is not just the task of a special group within a company; employees of all levels, from the CEO down, participate in kaizen activities. When the kaizen philosophy is applied, every single organizational member is responsible for the improvement processes. Another feature of kaizen is that every process, not only a manufacturing or a service process, can be improved, which means that kaizen can also be applied in nonmanagerial situations. For example, if a Westerner wanted to avoid drinking coffee anymore, he or she would make a radical change in drinking habits, trying to completely stop consuming coffee from one day to the next. However, this might not be successful since the body is not accustomed to a lack of caffeine. This might then affect the mood and work abilities of the person. However, if the kaizen attitude is applied in this situation, the person might first substitute one cup of green tea for a cup of coffee on the first day. This is a first step in making the change, and the person still feels well and the body can adjust to the change in the amount of caffeine consumed. A day or a week later, two cups of coffee per day are substituted with green tea, and after awhile, switching entirely to green tea is very easy.

The following sidebar (Implementing Kaizen) describes in which way a kaizen-oriented attitude can be implemented within Western organizations.

Implementing Kaizen

- Encourage a corporate culture in which new ideas are rewarded and employees are interested in improvements.
- Promote shared responsibility; all employees, from top management down, are responsible for improving business processes.
- Stress that even small processes can be improved.
- Remember that starting with a small step (e.g., one cup of green tea a day) lowers resistance to change and helps employees to adjust to new ideas.
- Hold regular reflection meetings about the regular progress in which improvements are discussed and promoted.

The 5S System

Another famous management practice related to gemba kaizen is the 5S System. The "5S" refers to five key words all starting with an "S" in Japanese. The words describe how a workplace or production process can be effectively organized. The 5S System consists of five stages of a production process, which are *seiri* (sort), *seiton* (set in order), *seiso* (clean), *seiketsu* (systematize), and *shitsuke* (standardize). The words combined do not really make up a system but a set of guidelines regarding how to improve a business or production process, or any kind of standardized process, and maintain lasting, high-quality performance.

In the first stage, *seiri*, all tools and materials used in the work process are taken care of. *Seiri* refers to tidiness and structured organization. During the *seiri* process, all materials and tools are sorted, and only the necessary ones are kept for continued use. Everything else is stored or discarded. This process leads to fewer hazards and less clutter that might interfere with productive work.

Stage 2, *seiton*, refers to straightening and orderliness. In this phase, all the materials and tools chosen for the production process are organized. The focus is on the need for an orderly workplace. Even though the translation appears to indicate something similar to "sweeping," the intent is to arrange the tools, equipment, and parts in a manner that promotes workflow. It has to be systematic. For example, tools and equipment should be kept where they will be used (i.e., in order to straighten the flow path), and the process should be arranged in an order that maximizes efficiency. There should be a place for everything, and everything should be in its place—this is also known as "demarcation and labeling of place."

Stage 3, *seiso*, stands for sweeping and cleanliness. It means to clean all items used at work (e.g., all materials used during a manufacturing process). The workplace, for example, has to be clean and tidy all the time. At the end of each shift, a work area is cleaned up and everything is restored to its place. This makes it easy to know what goes where and to have confidence that everything is where it should be. The key point is that maintaining cleanliness should be part of daily work—not an occasional activity that is initiated only when things get too messy.

Phase 4, *seiketsu*, translates as "standards." *Seiketsu* refers to making all the cleaning, control, and improvement processes a regular activity in the workplace, allowing for control and consistency. Basic housekeeping standards apply everywhere in the facility. Everyone knows exactly what his or her responsibilities are. Housekeeping duties are part of regular work routines.

Phase 5, *shitsuke*, means "sustaining discipline." It also refers to standardizing and sustaining the process to support long-term *kaizen* goals and to maintaining and reviewing standards. Once the previous four phases have been established, they become the new way of operating the organization. Maintaining a focus on this new way of operating is essential, and a gradual decline back to the old ways of operating should not be allowed. But if an issue arises about improvements in working, a new way of doing things, or a new requirement concerning output, it usually leads to a review of the first four commandments.

In a Japanese context, a sixth phase, "safety," is sometimes added. Purists, however, argue that adding this phase is unnecessary since correctly following 5S will result in a safe work environment. Often, however, a poorly conceived and designed 5S process can result in increases in workplace hazards when employees attempt to maintain cleanliness at the expense of ensuring that safety standards are adequately followed.[2] In Table 1.1, we can see an overview of the 5S System.

Table 1.1. Overview of the 5S System

5S system	Activity
seiri (sort)	Materials and parts used in the production process are sorted and the unused parts are stored at another place.
seiton (set in order)	Parts chosen are put in order and organized; things are kept tidy and in a certain order.
seiso (clean)	In this stage, all parts, as well as the workplace, are cleaned.
seiketsu (systematize)	All processes become regular activities at the workplace in order to guarantee consistency and reliability in quality and results.
shitsuke (standardize)	The first four Ss become the new way of operating the production process. In the fifth stage, all processes developed in the first four stages are standardized and communicated to all employees in order to support kaizen goals.

Total Quality Management, Japanese Style

Japanese consumers are obsessed with quality and do not accept any product defects. In the case of a product defect, the product will be returned, but the Japanese customer is lost forever. To avoid any problems with quality, decades ago, Japanese corporations started improving and refining their production management processes (see *jidôka* in chapter 3) and also implemented a number of instruments for controlling and sustaining quality at the highest level.

Quality, however, plays an important role in all the other business processes as well. Here again, as with the kaizen approach, the quality idea is relevant at every level and stage. Total quality control is implemented in all phases of the manufacturing and work processes, and it is not simply result oriented. While working employees are constantly expected to check and improve the quality of work, mistakes must be reported or fixed as soon as they are found. Japanese firms apply a number of interesting tools to leverage their employees' creativity and ideas and to make sure that their products and services are produced at the highest level. The most prominent tools are described in the following sections.

Quality Circles

The concept of quality circles is based on the idea that the interaction between different members of a group is more productive than several individual ideas. A Japanese quality circle is a small group, usually consisting of 8 to 10 people from the same work area, who are voluntarily involved in studying and solving product-quality problems. The problems they deal with are either problems that need improvement that the members find important or problems that the company assigns to them to solve. In her book *The Accidental Office Lady*, Laura Kriska describes her time as an American working for a well-known Japanese carmaker. At the time, women working in an office had to wear uniforms, while men did not. After complaining about this, Kriska was told to form a quality circle and present suggestions for improvement. A group formed and collected data on costs, motivation, and other factors, and after a few months, the results, which suggested that the uniform rule should be abandoned, were presented to the top management. The presentation was convincing, and the company changed its policy.

This example shows that every area of the workplace is a target for possible improvements and that a group-oriented solution is preferred. When developing solutions within the quality circle, the well-being of all company members is of the highest importance and should be considered at all costs. Training plays an important role in quality circles. The circle leader is first trained by the senior management and then devotes a remarkable amount of time and energy to disseminating statistical knowledge and other related expertise to his or her subordinates (during the normal work time or in their spare time). The consequence is more worker participation and positive group dynamics, as every member is equipped with the relevant knowledge and skills and can freely communicate his or her ideas.

Thus, the existence of quality circles significantly improves product quality as well as productivity. Also, however, individual suggestions must not be neglected. Suggestions given by circle members strongly stimulate innovation in Japanese firms, and members are encouraged to register patents in case the group discussion leads to inventions or new products.

Genchi Genbutsu (Go and See)

Genchi genbutsu, a Japanese term translated into English as "go and see for yourself," has revolutionized Japanese firms and their business practices. This phrase enforces a simple but effective policy where employers immerse themselves in their company's daily operations by experiencing a production site or business section for themselves. Genchi genbutsu is used to train young employees who are entering the company right after graduating from a university to let them experience the work and learn it from scratch. Many Japanese companies have a strong focus on stability and prefer their workforce to remain constant for many years, sometimes even a lifetime (see chapter 2). They usually take 1 or 2 years to train their employees and socialize them in the firm. In most cases, this happens also by genchi genbutsu. A new recruit entering a Japanese sales department will accompany a more experienced sales manager for up to 2 years before visiting a customer alone for the first time. This allows him to learn the business from a more experienced person; to become familiar with the customers, their likes, and their dislikes; and to become accustomed to the business. After being socialized in this manner, employees feel more relaxed doing their jobs and show greater motivation.

Genchi genbutsu is also used in cooperation with job rotation, which is still very popular in the Japanese firm (see chapter 2). Many Japanese employees are moved to a new department every 2 to 3 years to ensure that they know all aspects of the business. In their new assignment, they learn each task by doing it from scratch. Japanese top managers who mostly "grew up" in only one firm have often worked in almost all parts of their company and really "know every corner of the firm." This is one reason why Japanese firms feel uncomfortable hiring top managers from other firms or industries. The tacit and personal knowledge that can be acquired by genchi genbutsu is considered priceless and makes all employees experts in all aspects of their business over time.

The hands-on approach of genchi genbutsu is also used to improve processes and solve problems. "Let us go back to the gemba, or the shop floor, and look for solutions there," is a Japanese slogan when there is a problem that needs to be solved and the solution is not visible right away.

Reflection Meetings

Another tool for improving quality at a constant level is the reflection meeting, called *hanseikai*, which is held after projects, events, or any task that is performed by a group. A hanseikai is a very traditional way of reflecting on a project and implementing changes for future performance. In this meeting, the task is very carefully discussed by all team members, and possible improvements are developed during this discussion. A Japanese task is not finished until the hanseikai is over. A *hanseikai* usually consists of three components. In the first step, all team members analyze the task and compare the initial project plan to the actual performance. Following the first step, the performance of each team member is discussed, and they reflect on their own performance and make suggestions on how they could improve it next time. Finally, there is a feedback round in which the group discusses the particular aspects that could be improved and that need to be considered in future projects.

Since a hanseikai can last a few hours, it is held right after the end of a task, when memory is still fresh and all members have ideas about how to improve the processes in the future. They recognize the company's weaknesses, and they must be responsible for changing and fixing those weaknesses. A *hanseikai* is a management tool that is deeply embedded in Japanese culture.

Summary

- Kaizen is the most prominent Japanese management practice. It refers to continuous improvement and the idea that any managerial process can be perfected. Kaizen is not so much a detailed management practice but a philosophy that should be lived and implemented by every member of a Japanese firm, from the top management to the shop floor. The idea of kaizen does not include radical changes, such as job cuts, but mostly consists of small changes, often on a daily basis, and is based on constant communication with other group members.
- The 5S system is system consisting of five concepts that begin with the letter "S" in Japanese: *seiri* (sort), *seiton* (set in order), *seiso* (clean), *seiketsu* (systematize), and *shitsuke* (standardize). The 5S system is an organizational system for production processes.
- Quality circles are a means of quality management in the Japanese firm. They support employees in contributing their own ideas.
- Genchi genbutsu refers to inspection at the level of the shop floor. In doing this, Japanese employees can find solutions for problems at the actual place where they occur.
- After a project or an event, Japanese business people usually hold a reflection meeting called *hanseikai*. In a *hanseikai*, the performance is evaluated, and points of improvement are discussed.

CHAPTER 2

Human Resource Management

Japanese management is strongly related to the country's unique culture, which was formed and strengthened by a century-long seclusion of the country. Confucianism is the base of Japanese culture and society, and its influences can also be observed in Japan's business practices today. Japanese corporations have developed very unique human resource management practices, such as lifetime employment, job rotation, and a strong focus on training within the firms. These practices are often called the backbone of Japanese economic development, since they supported the rapid economic development of the country after World War II. And even if many Japanese human resource practices are challenged by economic development, many of them are still practiced in the Japanese firm. This chapter provides an overview of the most prominent Japanese human resource practices and their relevance for the modern Japanese firm. Upon completion of this chapter, you should be able to understand the following:

- How relationships in a Japanese firm are structured
- What aspects are important in Japanese company communication
- How the background of lifetime employment is important and why it is relevant
- How the seniority principle works in the Japanese firm
- What *madogiwazoku* are
- Why Japanese companies have a tendency to rotate the employees
- How Japanese trade unions differ from Western unions
- What trends dominate Japanese human resource management today

Group Orientation in the Japanese Firm

Japan is a collectivistic culture, which means that the well-being of the whole team is more important than the well-being of one individual. Westerners often assume that Asian people secretly prefer to be more individualistic and (especially when working in a Western firm) are only looking for opportunities to do so. However, this is not quite correct. In general, being in a group or team is considered better than performing things on one's own. In Asian societies, being a member of group is considered more positive and valuable than being a nonmember (even if this means that one can fulfill one's personal wishes and intentions). Being in a group comes with comfort and security. Japanese groups and teams also resemble families, accepting people's differences but expecting them to behave in a certain way.

Japanese teams exhibit some very special features. Membership in a team or organization is extraordinarily important; teams clearly distinguish between members and nonmembers (*uchi-soto*). In an organizational context, full-time employees get not only job security but also all benefits, including health insurance, a pension plan, and bonuses, whereas part-time workers lack all of these. Once a person enters a Japanese organization, he or she is expected to stay for a long time (often resulting in a lifelong relationship) and is screened very carefully before being hired. Leaving a team or organization can be very difficult and may be considered abandonment of other members of the company.

Japanese groups (and organizations) are difficult to enter and to leave. In order to study at a prestigious university or to work for a well-known Japanese firm, young people are required to spend years studying and to go through a very difficult and extremely competitive recruiting process. Once they have entered a company, however, they will benefit from the security of their firm and will be considered members of these organizations for most of their lives.

Japanese teams and organizations are organized vertically. This means that older members have more power, earn more, and are considered more knowledgeable, even if this is not really the case. In schools, companies, and other organizations, the *senpai-kôhai* (senior-junior) system is still in place. Older members of an organization not only are shown very high respect but also are responsible for socializing younger employees into the company's doings and training them. Senpai-kôhai relationships can last a lifetime.

Japanese groups and companies have a long-term orientation. Team members should have a good or friendlike relationship with one another. Harmonious relationships have a high priority; open conflict and competition are mostly avoided. To guarantee harmonious cooperation, Japanese prefer to stick to rules and clearly defined procedures. Detailed processes dominate the Japanese workplace. In many famous Japanese management areas, such as production management (the famous "Toyota way," for example) and the service industry, Japan's obsession with process has led to world leadership in these areas. However, Japanese firms are very often criticized for not being strategic or future-oriented enough, concentrating too much on management operations and internal relationships, and often neglecting strategic aspects.

Japanese groups and organizations always exhibit high motivation and are oriented toward high achievement. Working hard and doing one's best are strongly promoted values in Japanese society. There are two main concepts that describe this attitude. *Ganbaru* refers to pulling things through, such as bringing a difficult task to its end regardless of hardship or troubles. *Gaman* refers to the ability to endure things one cannot change, such as a 1- or 2-hour commute in a very crowded train every morning to get to work.

Entering a Japanese Organization

Japanese groups, teams, and organizations make a clear distinction between inside and outside or members and nonmembers. This principle is called *uchi-soto* (inside-outside).

Uchi, or inside, refers to people inside one's family or organization. Group members get all the benefits from the group or organization they belong to. In an organization, this would refer to health insurance, a pension plan, a commuting and rent allowance, and often the assurance that one will work in the company for a lifetime. Many aspects of the employees' lives are taken care of by the company. Being relieved from potential fears about their professional future, employees are expected to dedicate themselves, with all their heart, to the well-being of the group.

Soto refers to people who do not belong to the organization—that is, they are nonmembers. These individuals play a less important role in a Japanese person's life. The utmost attention is given to individuals who belong to one's family, school, or company. The clear distinction between insider and outsider can also be observed in Japanese firms, which draw very clear lines between full-time employees and nonemployees (or part-timers, who are also considered nonmembers). The *uchi-soto* principle also explains why Japanese companies are traditionally very reluctant to lay off their employees and remove them from their organizations. Membership in any Japanese organization comes with a lot of benefits, such as job safety and a secure future for one's family. A lifetime job in a Japanese company is not only a sign of success—having this type of job allows employees to start building their lives in Japanese society. It allows them to marry, get a loan, and secure the financial future of their children.

The *uchi-soto* principle also influences employee relationships with people and organizations outside the company. Such relationships are certainly friendly but are often less important (except for clients). Relationships with partner firms are dominated by professional respect and by a hierarchy in which all participants are connected with each other.

The *uchi-soto* form of respect is the reason why membership in a group is so important in Japan. However, very prestigious groups, such as famous universities or large Japanese multinationals such as Toyota, are very difficult to enter. From a very early age, young people in Japan try to enter a well-known high school and, consequently, a university that will enable them to enter a prestigious firm upon graduation.

Because group membership must be earned, attempting to enter a group is often a time-consuming and tiresome effort. Japanese groups choose new members very carefully, sending them through numerous procedures in order to test their personalities before accepting them into their group. After an individual overcomes the difficulties and severity of an entry process and becomes a member of a certain organization, his or her life immediately improves. The race to enter and then secure membership in a successful organization is extremely competitive, but once a student succeeds and enters a prestigious company, he or she could assume to stay there for the rest of his or her career. The relationship between the individual and the group or organization is long lasting and reliable.

The competition to enter prestigious groups, such as famous universities or companies, starts at a very early age. Japanese children compete from the time they enter primary school through their high school years for places in prestigious schools and, finally, for a place in one of Japan's top universities. It is hoped that this trajectory will lead to a job in a famous firm, promising lifetime employment. Relationships with their fellow classmates and professors, which are developed during the school and university years, last a lifetime and ultimately support their careers. Applicants are required to take an entrance examination, which often requires years of preparation. Students study for many years to pass the entrance exam, similar to the process that awaits graduates when seeking to enter a famous multinational corporation. Japanese companies, especially companies with a good reputation, are extremely difficult to enter. They mostly hire graduates who, in their final year at the university, spend many stressful months taking tests and interviewing to find a job in a well-known corporation. Once they are inside one of these companies, they can stay there for many years to come. They may be required to spend a lot more time working than Western employees would, but in most cases their jobs are safe for the long term.

Leaving a Japanese team or organization is often as difficult as entering, and it comes with major negative consequences. It is considered suspicious when a person decides to leave a job at a famous company, even if offered a better position at another firm. Many Japanese people regard this as a disloyal act. Changing jobs and midcareer hiring were quite unusual in Japan until a few years ago. Japanese companies are not very well equipped to integrate new members who have not been with them since right after their graduation. Upon leaving, people lose all the relationships they had built in the firm.

Entering a Western group or organization is, in many cases, easier than in Japan. The distinction between group members and nonmembers is not as strong. Group members often follow individual goals rather than group goals. If they prefer to leave the group, they can do so without major social consequences.

Relationships Within the Firm

To be effective and to be competitive, Japanese teams exhibit a very strong and solid group structure. Japanese groups are based on seniority, where older and more experienced members have more influence on other members. Older members of the group are considered more experienced and have more power. They are called *senpai*, and not only do they have more power, but they also have numerous duties. Since relationships play a major role in Japanese firms, older members are responsible for younger employees and their training, so they help them become integrated into the organization. Younger employees are called *kôhai*; they are expected to follow the advice of their *senpai* and to show respect for them. *Senpai-kôhai* relationships can last a lifetime and can be found in every Japanese elementary school as well as in the largest businesses in Japan. Even *senpai* who are only a year older will be shown respect and obedience. *Senpai* is often translated as "mentor" in English, but the Western concept of mentorship greatly differs from the Japanese. *Senpai* and *kôhai* are connected to each other in a parent-child type of relationship. *Senpai-kôhai* relationships last for a long time—sometimes a lifetime. They are based on trust and a shared responsibility for all group members. Every member of the group therefore has a position and can relate very easily to other members of the group. A *senpai* is responsible for advising *kôhai* and for supervising their actions in the group or organization. The kôhai, on the other hand, shows a *senpai* great respect by reacting to his or her suggestions and addressing him or her with highly honorific language.

In the Japanese firm, this relationship becomes obvious in most business processes. Every member of a Japanese firm is a *senpai* and a kôhai at the same time. There are always older and younger team members. Both are entangled in lifelong relationships, which can never really be abandoned. The *senpai-kôhai* system is an integral part of Japanese societal structure and a seniority relationship system that plays an important role in Japanese management. The *senpai-kôhai* system is not only the foundation of power—it is also considered part of the compensation employees receive from their company.

In Western cultures, teams develop differently. Western groups also have hierarchical structures, but they are not always based on the principle of seniority. Many Western groups prefer horizontal rather than vertical relationships, and most Western groups also favor equality within the group. The position and experience of each member is more important than the length of an employee's stay in the firm.

Senpai-kôhai relationships invade all aspects of Japanese life. We can find it within families, schools, and universities as a strong fabric that organizes Japanese society. All Japanese are entangled in relationships with older and younger people and have to apply special behaviors toward members in each category.

Both *senpai* and kôhai have clearly defines roles in the relationship. The *senpai* guides the *kôhai* in both official and personal matters. In the workplace, the senpai provides on-the-job training and acts as a role model for the kôhai. This relationship helps the new employee to adapt to the company more easily and to develop a stronger devotion to work and to the firm. By supporting, teaching, and sharing experiences, a *senpai* and *kôhai* develop a strong personal bond.

Besides the emotional aspect, the *senpai* also supports the socialization process of the new employee. *Senpai* are the intermediaries between newcomers and the company and help them to adjust to the working environment and culture of the company through teaching and explaining things to them. They motivate newcomers and support them in becoming strong and motivated employees. A kôhai also learns by observing and copying the senpai. Moreover, a kôhai is also expected to serve and obey to the *senpai*. Being a good *senpai* is an important task in a Japanese firm, and being a responsible, protective, and selfless *senpai* is the ideal. After a few years, the *kôhai* will become a *senpai* and mentor newcomers. Having had a good *senpai* experience will support the task and provide the next kôhai with a good role model.

The senpai-kôhai system is like a relay race in which information, experience, and skills are passed from generation to generation in the company. Even when *senpai* retires from a company, the relationships with their kôhai are lifelong and can be counted on even if they no longer work at the same company.

Nonhierarchical Relationships

In the West, a classmate is merely a friend or someone who will graduate the same year in school. In Japan, *dôkyûsei* shares the same meaning as "classmate" in the West, but it is also applicable to the business world. *Dôryô* describes the relationships among a group of coworkers or colleagues who entered into a company at the same time, making them "same-year classmates" of that company. Relationships among *dôryô* are the only equal relationships in a Japanese business setting. These relationships are often the closest and earliest relationships formed in a company, as *dôryô* share a similar situation and are able to empathize with each other because of their similar status in the group or company. They are also allowed to speak more openly and use informal language when speaking to each other.

Lifetime Employment (*Shushin Koyo*)

During its success in the 1980s, Japanese management became famous for the fact that Japanese companies would give their employees full job security. Employees were expected to stay in the firm for most of their careers; in many cases, they would not even have any other job until their retirement. Lifetime employment was seen as a major success factor of Japanese companies at that time, leading to higher motivation and dedication of Japanese workers. This technique allowed Japanese firms to focus on long-term innovations without fearing high turnover and knowledge leaks.

Until a few years ago, a typical Japanese *salaryman* career looked like this: A university graduate entered a company right after graduating and after successfully passing a strict and complex application process. The new employee started working at the lowest salary level and performed only supporting and administrative tasks for the first few years. All procedures were taught by superiors (*senpai*) in the firm, and the learning process was mostly experienced based. The employee would most likely gain insight into all sections of the company and would perform all kinds of work for at least a short period of time. Employees often changed departments, and after a few years in the firm, they knew most business operations in the firm and had good contacts in most departments. The salary increased every year according to the time spent in the company and not when special achievements were observed. An employee's work would most likely be very time consuming, and he or she would hesitate to ask for a day off unless sick or a relative had passed away. Employees would spend time with the boss and other colleagues at after-work *nomi-kai* (drinking sessions), where both private and business issues were discussed. On occasion, business deals were even discussed with trade partners in this relaxed environment.

A Japanese worker typically would not want to change jobs. After spending several or many years in one company and working his way up to a good salary, he would be reluctant to undergo the process over again from the lowest level. In return for his dedicated service, he would get benefits from his company, such as bonuses, health care, status, social security, and of course, the possibility of staying in the same firm for most or all of his work life. In cases where an employee showed very special talents, the career ladder could lead up to the CEO level, but in most cases, it would not. However, even if the person did not become CEO, the salary would continue to increase until retirement age. Most Japanese would be expected to retire at the age of 65. When retiring, the person would receive a *taishokukin*, or a monetary bonus that could be as large as 36 months of salary, if the person had spent an entire career within the firm.

Strengths and Weaknesses of Lifetime Employment

Lifetime employment brings benefits and problems to the Japanese firm. The overall goal of the policy is to provide security and stability for the firm and also for its employees. In securing long-term jobs, the company creates a more relaxed atmosphere within the firm because employees do not have to worry about their future and can fully concentrate on their work. Another aspect is the fact that long-term projects (e.g., product or technology research) are supported by the fact that people will rarely change their jobs. In a Western firm, high turnover rates have a negative effect on many projects, where project leaders might suddenly change. In Japan, however, project teams rarely change, even when the project takes many years. In Japan's postwar development, this business method became a major reason for Japan's fast and successful industrialization.

A company also provides all kinds of benefits for its full-time employees, such as health insurance, a pension plan, bonuses, and sometimes even housing. Despite the fact that people cannot be fired, lifetime employment does not have a negative effect on motivation in a Japanese firm. Since the group consciousness within a Japanese firm or team is so strong, all members will try to do their best, simply to be a good employee and team member. In most Japanese offices, up to 50 people work in one room, and people's performance is controlled by the fact that there is always another person nearby.

Lifetime employment also has its weaknesses. Generally, Japanese firms create a lot of generalists. Most employees are rotated around the firm and experience internal training. They often do not develop specific skills in a certain field. And even today, Japanese employees who do change jobs are often the ones that were not good enough to get a position in one of Japan's famous companies that do provide lifetime employment. This is especially a problem for foreign firms in Japan, which—unless they are not a multinational player with a well-known brand name—find it very difficult to hire specialists in almost every field.

Lifetime employment goes hand in hand with the seniority-based compensation system in Japan. This means that employees receive a low salary at the beginning of their careers but a relatively high salary once they have reached the age of 50. In other words, employees are cheap when they are young and have higher productivity. The older, and maybe less productive, they become, the more expensive they become as well. This difference was a major hurdle that Japanese companies faced during the recession in the 1990s. Their costs were extremely high because many of their employees were in their mid-40s.

There is no job market for top managers in Japan. Most Japanese top managers are raised in only one firm. They work their way up within their firm until they are assigned to lead the company. Until they reach the top, they often have worked in many different departments of the firm, so they know it really well, but they have rarely seen another company or industry.

Legal Aspects

Lifetime employment is not a Japanese law, but it is supported by the Japanese labor laws, which make it extremely difficult to fire full-time employees. In a Japanese firm, a new hire does not always get a contract but rather a job notification called a *jirei*. The *jirei* announces the beginning of the relationship between employee and corporation but does not exactly specify the job. Once employees have entered the firm, they receive a manual in which the rules and regulations of the firm are described, but in most cases, the company moves them through many different departments during their careers. This is the reason why there are almost no job descriptions for new hires in Japan.

This system has a negative consequence. If an employee cannot fulfill the job or is not integrating well into the team, there is very little chance to remove this person from the organization. Since the work content is not explicitly written in the contract, the company can in many cases not fire a person for incompetence or mistakes. Japanese labor laws only allow layoffs when a company is about to go bankrupt or in some other severe cases, such as a criminal offense by the employee. Laying off people therefore becomes a major problem for the Japanese firm not only in times of economic crisis but also in cases when an employee is clearly not suited for the job or damages the firm.

Madogiwazoku

The only way to limit the influence of employees who would be fired in a Western environment is to ostracize them from teams and let them know that they are not welcome anymore. These people become *madogiwazoku*, translated as "window-seat people" and referring to redundant or uncooperative employees who, instead of being dismissed, are assigned a position of virtually no importance or responsibilities.

Madogiwazoku are often portrayed as harassed and bullied outsiders, who experience the cruelty of the Japanese system. In Japanese company life, however, troublemakers are difficult to deal with. They can often not be dismissed and still have to be paid. The "seat next to the window" is a bit of a cliché as well—in reality, in order to decrease the problems that they may create, these employees are simply not allowed to attend any meetings or to take over any tasks. Often, the company can only wait until these employees decide to leave the firm.

Part-Timers on the Rise in Japan: Is This the End of Lifetime Employment?

As the economic situation in Japan has been quite challenged over the past few years, not every graduate has been able to land a job in a major company. The seniority system makes it more difficult to enter a firm at a later stage, and graduates need to find a job right after graduation. Not finding a job is a serious issue. First of all, this means that the student will have to wait another year to be able to join a company and will have to compete with the next round of graduates. Companies do not react very openly to "leftover" graduates, and in many cases, leftover graduates will not find a job at all.

The time pressure that university students face to find a job is also one of the reasons that Japanese university students rarely study overseas and that the number of exchange students being sent overseas from Japan is quite low. Often, the schedules of their partner universities are not compatible with the Japanese system, and they may lose a year and study 5 instead of 4 years, a fact that will make the job-hunting process a lot more challenging and often less successful.

Freeters and Hakensha

Graduates who are not able to enter full-time employment in a firm only have the option to work part time. Part-time jobs (often called *baito*), however, greatly differ from full-time positions in Japan. They have no job security, pay a lot less, and their holders will not receive any bonuses, a pension plan, or national health insurance. The Japanese refer to young people who never manage to get out of their part-time status as freeters, from the English word *free* and the German word *arbeiter* (worker). Discussions involving the concept of *freeters* are very emotional in the Japanese media because the idea of not contributing to a company in a full-time manner is considered shameful by many Japanese.

Another type of worker that is growing in Japan is the *hakensha*, or contracted worker. The number of work agencies renting out workers has risen over the past several years. However, the status, payment, and future prospects of *hakensha* are as dim as of that of *freeters*.

NEETS

Some young people in Japan do not enter the workforce at all. They either do not feel fit for the rat race of a traditional Japanese career, where a major part of life is dedicated to the company, or simply did not manage to find a job. A growing number of young Japanese therefore become NEETs, or persons who are "not in employment, education, or training." In general, this term refers to young people aged between 16 and 24 who left or dropped out of school or college. The number of NEETs is rapidly increasing. In Japan, 490,000 workers became NEETs in 2001, and this number has risen even more, up to 640,000 NEETs in 2006, and 984,000 in the first part of 2010. In 1993, 53% of NEETs were under 25, but now 61% are between the ages of 25 and 34.[1]

There are few factors influencing the NEET phenomenon. Recent generations who see their parents, specifically their fathers, working very hard and dedicating themselves to the well-being of their companies often leaves them unwilling to go through the same process. On the other hand, parents may not want their children to struggle in the same way as they did, so the children are not pushed as hard as their parents were.

In struggling with this national problem, the government has set aside 37 billion yen (US$350 million) for programs to help the young secure jobs. These programs provide job-training sessions and will help young people to complete their resumes and find suitable jobs.[2]

Seniority Principle (*Nenko Joretsu*)

The seniority principle (*nenko joretsu*) is also visible in the Japanese firm. But while socially seniority is determined by age, in the company, seniority is determined by the year of entry in a company. An employee who is 26 years old and has worked for a company for only 2 years would be junior to the coworker in the same department who is 25 years old but has worked for the company for 4 years.

Nenko joretsu can still be found in most traditional Japanese firms. When entering the firm, all employees start with the same salary, which is increased every year in April. There is no need to renegotiate the salary, even if one remains in the same firm for his or her entire career. Most Japanese firms have compensation categories, and each employee moves up these categories year by year. There is usually no big secret about how much people earn. There may be differences according to firm, where more famous firms pay more, but within one firm, the system is fair and leaves no room for jealousy or discrimination.

The company has advantages from this as well. Both employees and employers know when promotions are coming and are better able to plan and budget for the future of both the individual and company. Employees are less likely to change companies (out of fear of losing their current status upon moving from the current employer) and in turn, employees are very future oriented and believe that if they stay with the company, they will have financial stability.

One of the first issues with *nenko joretsu* is the aging population of Japan. As Japanese employees become older, companies have more and more financial responsibility for their retired employees. This means that the financial burden to pay out retirement money rests with younger employees, and the company's expense becomes larger. Because of this, Japanese firms now tend to hire more part-timers. But since part-timers are not integrated very well into a seniority-based system, their dedication is lower than that of full-time employees.

Nenko joretsu also leads to a lack of specialists within a company. The system itself is designed to enable companies to give workers all-around experience by placing them in different departments or divisions during their tenure with the company. While this gives each worker the ability to do many different jobs and is a very effective "cover" system when an employee takes time off, it also prevents any employee from becoming a true specialist in any field.

Trade Unions

In Japan, the members of an enterprise union include all white-collar and blue-collar workers of a single company. There is usually only one union in one firm, and only a few labor unions in Japan connect members of one industry or trade; most unions are in-house unions. Until a few years ago, the labor union was mainly concerned with negotiating wage increases with the firm. In general, the union has the power to call for strikes, but this power is rarely executed. The relationship between the company and enterprise union is such that both entities are willing to cooperate for a common interest. The idea of harmony dominates the cooperation. Since all workers belong to the same union, the management cannot set one group against another. However, if the union's activities are too vigorous and disruptive, then the overall damage may actually come at the union members' own cost. As a result, vocal demonstrations are mostly held during lunch breaks or after working hours, and unless there appears to be a total breakdown in trust and labor unrest, strikes are mostly avoided. Another interesting aspect is the custom that having a major management role in the union often supports a manager's position in the firm, which is considered good management training. It is not uncommon that company union leaders also become high-level executives in the same company.

The role of Japanese trade unions has changed over the years. As the appeal of lifetime employment and seniority promotion has started to wear thin for young Japanese workers, talented employees are now less willing to invest in a career in which they are trapped with hard-to-sell company-specific skills. As a result, the role of enterprise unions has gradually shifted from collective bargaining to consultation. Furthermore, with new types of unions appearing, especially support groups for foreigners and part-time workers, Japanese trade unions are changing and taking on more tasks similar to their Western counterparts.

Training

Training for a Lifetime

In a Japanese firm, a new employee, most commonly a new graduate, is not required to know anything about the firm, but will receive training and education from the company. The idea of on-the-job training is carried out in Japanese companies with the assumption of lifetime employment. Training a new employee with potential is viewed as an investment to the firm.

Experience-Based Learning

The Japanese firm educates newcomers simultaneously in order to equally prepare them for their jobs in the company. Training is conducted in order to obtain knowledge and acquire the necessary skills. Training can be formal, or it can be informal, accomplished by daily social contact with instructors, supervisors, and senior members in the organization. *Senpai*—older employees—play a major role in training and socializing younger employees into their roles in the firm. "Learning by doing" is a common teaching method. In their first year, employees are required to watch and learn by copying their superiors. It is only after a few years—after they have grown into their roles and learned all of their tasks from scratch—that they are allowed to perform work more independently.

Job Rotation (*Haichi Tenkan*)

One of the training techniques utilized in the Japanese corporation is job rotation. Job rotation is a system that rotates the employees around different divisions of the company. *Haichi tenkan*—a distinctive characteristic of Japanese management—is the redistribution or relocation of the employees within the same firm or organization. This method enables each employee to understand and perform the tasks in different divisions. By rotating jobs, the employees will be able to experience different sectors of the company and be able to learn various skills. This exposure will allow employees to attain a variety of skills in order to enhance job satisfaction and to cross-train. Although this prevents the employees from developing specialized skills, it will enable them to become multifunctional workers and understand the company as a whole. More than 60% of Japanese firms—and over 80% of banking, financial, and insurance firms—practice haichi tenkan.

Haichi tenkan allows workers to familiarize themselves with the tasks of different departments in the firm. Therefore, the flexibility of the workers in the firm increases and employment adjustments are easily made. For example, a company can rotate and rearrange its human resources according to the economic environment in order to keep up with the pace of changing market requirements.

Haichi tenkan also allows employees to remain competitive. Nowadays, technology changes rapidly, especially in Japan. With *haichi tenkan*, workers are able to acquire new and updated skills in their current jobs and to keep up with changing skill requirements in the industry.

This kind of retraining within the firm also insures workers against the uncertainty of skills required in future settings.

Summary

- All relationships within the Japanese firm are based on the seniority principle. Every team member is interwoven in a web of relationships in which older members have more power, higher status, and a higher salary than younger ones. Older members are called *senpai* and the younger ones are *kôhai*. *Senpai* have the responsibility of training and integrating younger members into the company. Kôhai are expected to show obedient behavior and support their superiors while learning a job from scratch. The seniority principle, which is a major pillar of Japanese society, can still be observed in Japanese corporations. Even if an increasing number of Japanese companies are considering more achievement-based measures for promotions and salary raises, seniority still plays a major part in how businesses in Japan are organized. The *senpai*-kôhai relationships still dominate the way people are trained in firms and influence all relationships in the *kaisha*, or firm.
- Lifetime employment is another enigma of Japanese success. Lifetime employment refers to the famous management practice in which Japanese firms hire new graduates and have them work in their firm until retirement. Lifetime employment is still considered the "fulfillment of the Japanese dream." Today, it has become a bargaining chip for companies to recruit talent for their corporations. On the other hand, the number of part-time employees is continuously increasing in Japan. Another phenomenon that is on the rise in Japan is the emergence of a class of individuals referred to as NEETs ("not in employment, education, or training"), who are young people who are still living with their parents and do not have a job.
- Japanese trade unions have traditionally played a different role in Japanese firms than their counterparts in the West. In Japanese firms, unions are dominant, and every big company usually has their own union. Until now, these unions were in

charge of negotiating annual wage increases with the firm, but they typically did not have much power. Over the past several years, they have turned to a more Western role and increasingly support their members who are facing part-time job issues and contract violations.

- Training activities occupy a major part of Japanese work life. Job rotation is another typical feature of Japanese human resource management. The reason for job rotation is the Japanese preference for functional organizational structure and their need to ensure that all employees experience all aspects of the company's business. Job rotation also creates strong identification with the firm as a whole rather than just a single department. This method also encourages employees to develop good relationships with their colleagues throughout the firm.

CHAPTER 3

Production Management

Japanese firms are world leaders in cost-efficient and quality-oriented manufacturing. Next to kaizen, Japanese production management techniques have had the greatest influence on Western firms and their business processes. Japanese firms have managed to make products for almost half the price of those of their Western competitors and have reduced the product defect rate to almost zero.

The leading firm in this field is Toyota, which is responsible for many groundbreaking techniques such as just-in-time management (or lean management), the so-called *kanban* system, and other successful concepts such as *jidôka* and *heijunka*. The overall goals of these techniques are to reduce any kind of waste and to improve the quality of production processes and the final products. Today, however, these practices have become a standard in Japanese firms, and they have moved beyond these practices to develop even more efficient manufacturing processes. Upon completion of this chapter you will be able to understand the following:

- What just-in-time management is and how it made Japanese firms successful
- How the famous *kanban* and *heijunka* systems work
- How Japanese manufacturers control quality in their production processes
- What trends can be observed in Japanese production management today

Process Orientation (*Shikata*) and Perfectionism (*Kanzen Shugi*)

Japanese organizations are a strong unit with a solid hierarchical structure. These groups also have very clear rules and expect all members to abide by them. To guarantee harmonius and long-lasting relationships, Japanese employees have developed a strong sense of duty and are very dedicated to their tasks. Rules and regulations play an important role in a Japanese workplace and must be followed at all costs to avoid problems for other team members. Japanese companies have therefore developed a very strong process orientation. All procedures in a Japanese firm are practiced very carefully and sequentially. This concept is called *shikata*, or the proper way of doing things. Japanese process orientation helped the Japanese economy develop very rapidly. Manufacturing and production processes have benefited from the positive attitude toward processes. Even today, there is a high degree of process orientation in Japanese service management.

Just-in-Time Management

Just-in-time (JIT) is a management philosophy based on planned elimination of all waste, such as inventory and associated carrying costs within production, essentially to improve a business's return on investment. It is a production strategy aimed at streamlining a production process by sending the right part to the right place on the manufacturing line at the right time. Just-in-time production techniques produce parts as they are needed in order to keep inventory low and minimize storage costs. Implemented correctly, JIT can dramatically improve a manufacturing organization's return on investment, quality, and efficiency. Just-in-time is the one Japanese management practice that has been most successfully implemented in Western corporations.

Elimination of Waste

Just-in-time management is based on the idea of eliminating all kinds of waste. In a production system, only a small fraction of total time and effort actually adds value for the customer. Once the value for the customer is clearly defined, eliminating waste means to eliminate nonvalue activities step by step in order to become more profitable.

Muda is a traditional Japanese term for anything not adding value for the customer. Eliminating this waste is an effective way of increasing profitability. *Muda* refers to various forms of waste. Overproduction is producing beyond customer requirements in the form of unnecessary materials and products. Reducing this waste increases the amount of space available for storing raw materials as well as finished goods. Another type of waste is unnecessary transportation, as every time a product is moved, there is a risk of its being damaged, lost, or delayed. Inventory, which is the purchasing of unnecessary raw materials of both works in process and finished works, is considered another form of waste. Unnecessary movements and products defects should also be avoided because they lead to overprocessing, unnecessary steps in the production process, and delays.

Muri is a traditional Japanese term for overburdening. *Muri* happens when processes and operators do not have sufficient time to carry out their work, affecting the whole process of flow. Overburden is considered a waste because it leads to inefficiency, resulting in safety and quality problems. If workers feel overworked and are then forced to make too many decisions, efficiency is reduced in the work in process in the form of time delays, task switching, and defects. At the same time, overburdening of equipment also causes breakdowns and defects.

Mura is a traditional Japanese term for unevenness. Mura occurs when products are batched together and pushed through a production plant. Widely varying the workload is a waste, since it has a direct impact on the productivity of manpower or materials. To ease the burden, jobs should be broken down into several tasks.

Heijunka

Another important concept of kaizen is production leveling, or *heijunka*. *Heijunka* aims to level out the work load of all work centers by producing roughly the same mix of products each day, using a repeating sequence in which several products are produced on the same line. With *heijunka*, production is constantly alternating between the different types, ensuring a constant flow of all products and shortening lead time. With *heijunka*, the variety of products made in one cycle reflects the actual demand for a product. This has the effect of reducing inventory.

At a company not using heijunka, inventory is large. If the company is making products in large batches, there will be a need for a large work-in-progress inventory for holding the large amounts of raw materials and there will be a large inventory of the same finished products at the suppliers' companies as well. This will increase costs.

Kanban

Just-in-time management is often also called the *kanban* system. Kanbans (or cards), however, are in fact a tool of just-in-time management. The cards are used to track parts during the manufacturing process and to ensure that the right parts are delivered to the right point in the production line in time. Each card contains information on the identity, origin, destination, and quantity of the parts.

Under the kanban system, no parts are produced until a production kanban is requested for them, and parts are produced exactly as the kanban specifies. Furthermore, only the exact number of parts requested is produced, even if production workers are idle between requests. To control inventory, managers determine how many kanban of each type are in use in the factory at any given time. In this way, managers can control the speed of production and adjust very quickly to changes in demand and the work environment. Since its introduction, the kanban system has been updated to make use of modern technology. Electronic kanban are now used, and a large amount of research and analysis has been done to determine the number of kanban needed to optimize the efficiency of the factory with a minimal inventory of parts. In addition, some companies with simpler manufacturing processes have combined electronic material requirements planning systems with the kanban system.

Jidôka

Japanese companies have always had an obsession with producing high-quality products without defects. In Japanese, *jidôka* literally means "automated" and refers to the automated procedures Japanese manufacturing companies would expect from their workers and assembly lines. Jidôka is a system that blocks defected products from penetrating the production line. The system is operated through inspections conducted by workers and by a device that immediately halts the entire production system when defective products are spotted. This is integral to the Japanese business world because jidôka represents the on-time, cost-effective, methodological ways in which they like to produce their goods to ensure that all goods are exactly the same and without fault. Not only is each manufacturing section equipped with automatic detectors that can identify when the product is abnormal, which will automatically switch off the entire procedure, but also each individual labor worker bears responsibility for quality checks for their specific sectors and can immediately stop the entire procedure when abnormality is manually detected.

Jidôka is a system in Japanese businesses that places people at an exact position so they can be responsible for a specific part of an entire product. It follows very precise procedures that demand everything to be working consistently from one step to another. In applying jidôka, the firm maintains a certain standard that is associated with both Japanese business products and services.

If jidôka is implemented in the way outlined here, there will be less need for a large number of workers to be assigned to one sector. Thus, the number of labor workers can be cut and then reassigned to do something else. As a result, as little as one person can be in charge of several machines, which will lower labor costs as well as smoothen the process of production. Work that can be done by machines will no longer be done by manual workers, and manual workers will only be asked to do jobs that are too complicated for machines. This type of labor division not only is cost effective for the company but also will increase the rate of production to further satisfy just-in-time needs.

In conclusion, we can understand jidôka as an integral quality-check process adopted by most, if not all, companies in Japan, especially those involved in manufacturing products. It is a check and recheck procedure that ensures the top quality of each product that is delivered to customers. It involves machines automatically detecting faults and individual workers being responsible for specific sections of the manufacturing process. Since the system heavily relies on physical inspections by individual workers, there is often great pressure on workers, which has been one of the labor issues at Toyota. Nonetheless, jidôka has systemized effective quality control, helping maintain Japanese corporations' reputation for high-quality products.

Trends in Japanese Production Management

Total Productivity Management

Many Japanese firms have implemented total productivity management (TPM) to achieve their corporate-wide targets. TPM works with a top-down approach and reduces a company's goals to tangible objectives and numerical targets for specific corporate activities. For example, if a company-wide goal required a 10% cut in production costs for a certain product, appropriate adjustments would have to be made all over the company. Steps within TPM are comprised of corporate goal setting, top-down enrollment, implementation, and assessment, and TPM is applied to the whole value chain, leading to changes throughout the entire company. The main differences between TPM and bottom-up approaches like TQM (total quality management) include the cost-reduction emphasis of TPM and the increased awareness by employees of the ways in which they contribute to the whole.[1]

Cell Production

Cell production is a new human-centered production system that replaces the traditional line system employed by many companies. There are various other terms for cell production, such as multitask spiral line or one-man production-line system. In the cell system, a single worker or small teams (up to five members) perform multiple production jobs in short segment lines. The cells are arranged in a U shape, and components enter close to the point where they leave as finished products. A wide range of tools and equipment is placed around the worker so he is able to perform various tasks as well as customize the products. It allows the production unit to react very flexibly to changes in demand. The cell system allows workers to produce small lots efficiently. The optimized cell design and highly skilled workers lead to increases in productivity. There are three basic types of the cell production system in existence.

One is the divided production system (*bunkatsu hôshiki*), where four or five people work in one cell and each of them performs specialized tasks. The second type is the one-man production system (*hitori hôshiki*), where one person performs all required tasks, including inspection, in one cell. The chase production system (*junkai* hôshiki) is the third type. It consists of two or three workers who perform all operations in turn and nearly at the same speed. The application of cell production is increasing and is often combined with the jidôka concept. It optimizes role sharing between workers and machines and leads to robot support in cell production. Through these methods, both quality and the efficiency of the workers can be increased. Robotics companies even offer robots that can completely substitute workers in a cell production system. The cell production system has been praised as less capital intensive, more flexible, better for the motivation of the workforce, more efficient, and more supportive in sharing knowledge between workers.[2]

Summary

- Just-in-time management (also called lean management or the Toyota production system) is the most famous Japanese management practice. A major goal of just-in-time management is the total elimination of waste.
- Heijunka assists in leveling out production and supports fast reactions to customer demand.
- Kanban refers to small cards that contain information about all the supply parts used in a production process. The *kanban* contains information on the part, how many are delivered, and where they need to go. The *kanban* is becoming a major part of the just-in-time manufacturing process.
- Today, Japanese car manufacturers have moved beyond the question of how to improve production processes, increasingly concentrating on new product development and increasing customer satisfaction and safety. The newest trends in Japanese production management include *total productivity management*, in which all departments of a corporation focus on cost saving, and *cell production*, a new, human-centered production system that replaces the traditional line system.

CHAPTER 4

Knowledge Management

Japanese companies focus very heavily on communication and free knowledge flow inside the company boundaries. In contrast to Western firms, there are few secrets within Japanese firms. Knowledge and information are shared freely within a firm because company goals are generally seen as more important than individual goals. Knowledge is not related to power because promotion and salaries are connected to an employee's age rather than to personal skills or achievements. Employees therefore do not need to develop career strategies based on individual knowledge. The Japanese way of managing knowledge has led to great advantages for firms when developing new products or implementing new and innovative technologies. Many of their techniques are very effective and can be implemented in Western corporations as well. Upon completion of this chapter you will be familiar with the following concepts:

- How Japanese knowledge management differs from approaches to managing knowledge in Western firms
- How knowledge flows freely in the Japanese firm
- How knowledge is created in Japan
- How Japanese companies develop new products

Knowledge Types in Japan

The most relevant distinction of knowledge is its division into the categories of tacit and explicit knowledge. Explicit knowledge is the most articulable type of knowledge, and it can be separated from its owner and expressed in formal and systematic language.[1] It is learned by observation and study[2] and shared in the form of data, scientific formulas, specifications, manuals,[3] patents, technical blueprints, computer software, and so on.[4] Because of its explicit form, it can easily be processed, transmitted, and stored.[5] As Western organizations prefer explicit knowledge, they prefer other types of knowledge management tools. A major goal of using these tools is to make explicit knowledge accessible to all members of the organization. Western organizations prefer explicit knowledge to tacit knowledge. The major reason for this attitude is the high turnover rate that characterizes Western firms. To make sure they can keep the expertise of their employees within the firm, they need to put this knowledge in a database and in documents and make it available to all members of the firm.

Japanese firms, on the other hand, prefer tacit knowledge, or knowledge that cannot so easily be put in words or other explicit forms. People may be able to perform certain tasks (e.g., riding a bicycle), but they may not be able to articulate the way they managed to perform these tasks. Being able to perform an activity does not imply that it is also possible to explain the very same action.[6] Tacit knowledge therefore not only is strongly connected to its knowledge owner but also is located within an individual. Japanese firms have a long tradition in dealing with tacit knowledge. Since most of their employees show high loyalty toward their firm and will stay in the company as long as possible, there is no need to extract their knowledge from them. Many processes in a Japanese firm are therefore not very well documented because older employees who know how to perform them are always present.

Knowledge in the Japanese Firm

Western organizations view knowledge management as a strategic issue that is supposed to improve company performance. Knowledge management activities are therefore often implemented and promoted by the top management. In Japanese organizations, however, knowledge management is already a vital part of daily processes. Managing and communicating knowledge involves all members of the organization, and the focus lies on how these processes can be improved and reach as many members of the organization as possible.[7]

Knowledge Management Is a Group Process

In Japanese firms, knowledge is created during group discussion processes. These processes are often circular and involve many aspects of the topic under discussion. Knowledge that is being created and used by all group members can therefore not be leveraged to increase an individual's power, only group power. In Western firms, however, knowledge is power, meaning individual power. The focus of knowledge creation lies in the discussion and comparison of individual ideas. Table 4.1 summarizes the differences between knowledge management in the East and West.

Knowledge Creation in the Japanese Firm

In Japan, the creation of knowledge is circular. Knowledge embodied in people is extracted and then communicated to other members of a group. In this way, knowledge is made accessible to all organizational members.

Table 4.1. Knowledge Management in Japan and in the West[8]

	Japanese knowledge management	Western knowledge management
Orientation	Group oriented	Individual oriented
Preferred knowledge type	Tacit knowledge	Explicit knowledge
Role of knowledge and knowledge management	Operational knowledge management (knowledge management processes)	Strategic knowledge management (knowledge as a strategic asset)
Knowledge and the individual	Knowledge is not a measure of individual's power	Knowledge is a measure of individual's power
Knowledge creation in the organizational context	• Redundancy of information • Creative chaos through overlapping tasks • Thoughts and feelings can be made explicit and thus communicated and shared	• Topic-oriented information • Creative chaos through individual differences • Knowledge creation is a continuous, self-transcending process
Philosophical view of knowledge	• Emphasis on experience • Unity of knowledge and action	• Emphasis on analysis • Knowledge as capital that can be valued

The shared knowledge is then internalized, and the cycle begins again. These interactions are referred to as *conversions*. The four modes of conversion are socialization, externalization, combination, and internalization. These four conversions are the basis of knowledge creation.[9] The model deriving from these four types of conversion is called the SECI model. The model describes the four conversion modes in terms of four forms of knowledge: tacit to tacit (socialization), tacit to explicit (externalization), explicit to explicit (combination), and explicit to tacit knowledge (internalization). Tacit knowledge is first turned into explicit knowledge by individuals, then by the group, and finally by the organization.

The first step in the SECI model is called socialization, in which existing tacit knowledge evolves into new tacit knowledge through shared experiences by individuals. An example would be gaining experience in sales negotiation. This could be easily achieved by accompanying an experienced salesperson for a certain period of time and observing how these negotiations are performed. In the socialization phase, individuals attempt to identify new knowledge by learning from their peers or mentors, and tacit learning happens through organizational practices such as mentoring and on-the-job training. Observation, imitation, and practice are other ways of learning instruments and work processes, which cannot always be put in words.[10] In gaining "real-life" experience, a young sales assistant can gain practical insights about the job, explore its particularities, and develop sensitivity for dealing with customers. Solutions for critical situations may also be developed during this on-the-job training. As a result, performance can be improved and staff members become more self-confident.[11]

In order to share this experience with other young salespeople in a corporation, this tacit and experience-based knowledge needs to be externalized. Accordingly, Nonaka (1994) calls the process of articulating tacit knowledge and transforming it into explicit knowledge externalization. Here, tacit knowledge is being made explicit in order to be shared with others.[12] Externalization can be achieved by involving techniques that help to express ideas or images as words, concepts, or figurative language such as metaphors, analogies, and narratives.[13] For example, trainees can process an experience during the on-the-job training by writing a presentation or a diary. Making tacit knowledge explicit, however, is not always easy. As described previously, tacit knowledge is highly personal and strongly reflects attitudes, feelings, or assumptions about a certain topic and, as such, is often very difficult to externalize.

Despite the difficulties of externalizing tacit knowledge, it is extremely useful for organizations. Once knowledge is made explicit, it can be distributed further. This process is called combination. This phase captures the idea that tacit knowledge and explicit knowledge are complementary but can expand over time through a process of mutual interaction.[14] During the combination process, explicit knowledge is created from explicit knowledge. Explicit knowledge is collected from inside or outside the organization and then processed into a new form of knowledge.[15] Individuals exchange and combine knowledge through mechanisms such as meetings and telephone conversations.[16] The experiences of a young sales representative, for example, could be used to train other young salespeople. After listening to a presentation about the experience, they can become more familiar with what to expect and can prepare themselves better. The knowledge gained in a tacit learning process and published in the form of a report may also be used in a manual for other future sales representatives. This information can address key questions and concerns about their future careers.

The final step in the SECI process is the conversion of explicit knowledge into tacit knowledge, which is referred to as internalization.[17] In this case, explicit knowledge that is being communicated throughout the organization is shared and converted into tacit knowledge.[18] A good example is a manual. For example, salespeople who read company manuals that explain critical sales situations may use this information on the job. By doing so, they internalize it and make it tacit again. The internalization process therefore bears some similarity to the traditional notion of learning,[19] and training programs are a very popular means of internalization. Knowledge that is internalized by the members of the organization in the form of shared mental models or technical knowledge is a valuable asset.[20]

New Product Development in Japan

One major field in which knowledge management is most important is the development of new products. Japanese product development teams are characterized by numerous features that allow them to take advantage of the creativity surrounding them.

Large Development Teams and Autonomy

In general, Japanese product development teams have more autonomy than their Western counterparts. This allows them to concentrate on their ideas without interference from top management. Japanese product development teams are often cross-functional and include numerous members from different departments of an organization. Another feature that increases the creativity of new product development is the integration of external experts who present different thinking approaches to the processes. An example is cooperation between corporations and *otaku* (enthusiastic consumers), which often leads to the development of new ideas.

Part of the reason for the successful development of new products is the highly dynamic Japanese market in which consumers constantly expect innovative goods. Japanese corporations have reacted to these expectations and have proved to be extremely successful in new product development.

Japanese corporate structure plays a major role in developing new products. Japanese organizations are typically characterized by a rather hierarchical structure with very rigid processes. In contrast to a Western organization, however, this structure does not lead to barriers in communication processes. Information and knowledge flows freely within Japanese organizations, which lays the foundation for effective new product development. On top of this, this type of structure leads to efficiently and diligently performed work processes, which lead to high quality and well-performed services. New product development processes in Japan are also characterized by these very particular features. Knowledge in a Japanese firm flows more freely than in a Western firm—since Japanese employees are more reluctant to leave their firms, tacit knowledge plays a more important role, and sharing knowledge is not as much a problem. When developing new products, the positive attitude toward sharing and the high relevance of tacit knowledge create a competitive advantage for the Japanese firm.

Open Office Space

Japanese office structure lays another foundation for successful new product development. Japanese offices often contain workplaces for up to 50 people, and the department boss usually has a desk in this room as well. From a Western perspective, where the corner office is still a status symbol, a large, open office with little distinction between higher and lower managers seems a bit daunting at the beginning. However, large office spaces improve and increase the communication of information between organizational members. New ideas can be communicated very easily and quickly, and of course, there is little room for secrecy or rumors.

Other places in which ideas may be shared are dinners or activities organized by the firm for employees. In Japan, it is very unusual to go out for just a drink or two after work—an evening out with team members always includes dinner. These dinners or drinking events are called *nomi-kai*, and these functions provide a forum for free communication and even criticism. They also allow employees to bond and create a stronger group orientation.

Large Development Teams

Japanese product development teams are built on the tradition of communicating directly within a large group. Such functions include a lot of different people, and it is important to get everyone's opinions and feedback. Even individuals who would not be relevant to the main development of a project or product are included and consulted from the beginning. A friend of mine working as an architect in Tokyo told me that when her firm starts planning a new project, even the craftsmen (such as carpenters) who are responsible for the tiniest details of the finishing of a building will attend the first meeting before the project is even properly drafted. They are asked for their opinion and are involved in the development of the building from the very first moment. As time consuming as this may be, the advantages of such processes are clear. All team members are informed about all happenings at all times, and can contribute with their specific expertise.

When developing new projects, Japanese teams also include researchers and consumers. In general, communications and exchanges between

Japanese companies and research facilities are very active, but apart from that, Japanese product development teams may also include enthusiastic consumers or other interest groups. The reason for the great variety of developers is the consideration of very different aspects and ideas when starting to develop an idea. In their book, Nonaka and Takeuchi suggest that tacit knowledge plays an important role in the product development stage. They refer to an employee who, even though working for a famous electronic manufacturer, worked a few months at a famous Osaka bakery to develop tacit knowledge on how to bake delicious bread. This knowledge was then used to develop a profit-creating bread-baking machine.[21]

Including Enthusiastic Consumers

Another source of knowledge increasingly consulted by Japanese product developers is enthusiastic consumers (*otaku*). Until a few years ago, otaku were seen as unsocial and even weird members of society, but their image has greatly changed. Companies now understand that these customers not only spend a lot more money on their products than the average consumer but also often know more about the products than the manufacturers' employees. Otaku are therefore increasingly involved and included in product development processes.

Individual Ideas as Group Ideas

If a team member (not only in a product development team but also in any other Japanese team) has a new idea, this idea will be consequently communicated to all group members. Any idea, no matter how small, becomes a group idea right from the start. This process differs from a Western discussion process. In a Western group, different opinions are verbalized, and team members try to convince each other to support a certain idea. In Japan, however, group discussion processes are more circular and surround a topic more than dissect it. The approach toward discussion is more playful, and every group member adds something to the topic. This allows even small ideas to grow and, at some point, to grow into something bigger.

Direct judgment is avoided at this stage and ideas are not dismissed very quickly, either.

Openness to Small Ideas

The group discussion in Japanese firms involves a high level of openness to new ideas and also helps identify ideas that would not be easily accepted in a Western environment. However, group discussions do have a downside. They smoothen the ideas to satisfy all members of the group. Radical or very dramatic changes will rarely be approved by all team members. This is one of the reasons why Japanese firms are very successful in taking Western ideas and "Japanizing" or improving them and why Japanese manufacturers are so successful with extremely customer-oriented products. This product-development style, then, does not allow for radical innovations.[22]

In a Western firm, product development processes are different. Here, groups also discuss ideas and improve them, but the idea starts with one individual. In most cases, this individual will be eager to ensure that he or she is recognized as the owner of the idea. In many cases, this employee will not share his or her idea with other group members right away. The reasons for this include a typically lower level of trust in Western firms (an idea might be stolen) and the wish to gain credit for the idea (in the form of either rights, bonuses, or promotion). In addition, an individual's idea will be screened by other members of the team or organization, which means it has to be presented in the best possible way and with great confidence. The owner of the idea will therefore develop the idea by himself or herself and prepare for criticism. The possibility of criticism helps one to sharpen the idea and strengthens the identification of the individual with the idea. The Western system also supports the development of very radical ideas that do not always seem feasible at the very beginning. This type of system also leads to a higher number of enthusiastic and creative entrepreneurs, such as Bill Gates, who really believe in their ideas and push them through all obstacles. Table 4.2 provides an overview of the differences between new product development in Western corporations and in Japan.

Table 4.2. New Product Development in Western Corporations and in Japanese Corporations

New product development in the West	New product development in Japan
• An idea is often developed by an individual. • An individual keeps the idea and develops it further (on his or her own). • The idea is only presented to other members of the group once its ownership is clear and it is resistant to major criticism. • Team members should be convinced of the idea, listening to it and then criticizing it to try to improve it.	• An idea is mostly developed by the group. • An individual places the idea on the group level right at the beginning. • The idea (even a small one) is communicated to other group members. • Team members circulate the idea within the group and improve and adapt it to mass market wishes.
Results of Western new product development	**Results of Japanese new product development**
• Radical innovations are possible and frequent. • The success of an idea depends on its owner; if the owner has a very entrepreneurial mind, the idea can be more successful.	• Radical innovations are less frequent; innovations developed in Japan target the mass market and tend to be more customer oriented. • Even a small idea has a chance; the success of an idea depends not on one individual but on how the group further communicates the idea.

The New Patent Law

Even in Japan, times are changing. No longer is every employee willing to hand over a profitable idea to his or her company. The Japanese patent law has responded to the changing attitude against traditional product development practices and now allows idea holders or creators to claim their rights and get part of the profit generated by their products. Over the past several years, Japanese courts have seen a number of lawsuits in which employees sued their employers and demanded to be compensated for their contribution to the firms. Many of these lawsuits included well-known firms such as Ajinomoto or Nichia, and these cases may have a long-lasting impact on the innovative capability of the Japanese firm.[23] It remains to be seen whether this law will have a major effect on how new Japanese products are being developed in the near future.

New Trends in Japanese Knowledge Management

Having survived the so-called lost decade, the recession in the 1990s, Japan's companies now face a completely new business environment. As new technologies enable new modes of communication between a company's employees, the use of social media in order to facilitate knowledge sharing has become widespread. These changes have strongly affected the way knowledge is managed in the modern Japanese firm.[24]

The most crucial issue in knowledge management today is the change in communication patterns. Personal communication and interaction was traditionally the basis of Japanese knowledge communication. Since most company members were expected to stay in their corporation for a long time, they could communicate freely and share knowledge without fearing negative consequences such as job loss. Japanese companies are aiming to reduce the number of meetings and the time they spend on decision making. At the same time, they lose time to interact and share ideas among employees.

Another competitive advantage of Japanese firms is their ability to create a strong unit of all employees. Due to frequent job rotation, departments within a Japanese firm play a less important role than the overall company. This feeling of oneness that most employees had in common allowed them to share ideas more freely, which led to highly customer-oriented products and an innovation-oriented atmosphere. Changing work patterns, such as an increasing number of job hoppers, less meetings, and the use of electronic media to communicate, has increased the focus on departments and teams and has led to a lower degree of knowledge shared among the organization's members.

Another aspect that used to be a strategic advantage of Japanese firms, but may become a strategic problem in the next few years, is their love of tacit knowledge. Today, many employees change jobs and take their tacit knowledge with them. Even when employees stay in one firm, they will eventually retire and will no longer be available to the firm. Many Japanese firms have therefore started to adopt

Table 4.3. Changes Regarding Knowledge Management in Contemporary Japanese Organizations[26]

Theory of organizational knowledge creation in the Japanese firm	Japanese knowledge management today
• (Tacit) knowledge experiences are shared with team members in the form of direct communication (frequent meetings) and nomikai (drinking events) or training on the job. • Informal meetings are a crucial aspect of the creation of new knowledge. • Intraorganizational knowledge creation and transfer via personal communication and interaction is a source of corporate success.	• Participation in informal after-work meetings and corporate activities outside work has declined due to higher work pressure and a shift in values. • Personal interaction in knowledge sharing is decreasing. • Less communication and interaction is occurring between different company units (departmental thinking increases). • The use of modern communication media, such as e-mail or mobile mail, has increased. Intranet and other databases allow exchange of explicit knowledge but cannot transfer context information.

knowledge-storing methods (e.g., databases and collections of best practices) from their Western competitors in order to keep knowledge within their firms and thereby sustain their competitive advantages.[25]

Summary

• Japanese knowledge management strongly focuses on tacit knowledge, that is, knowledge that is located in people and not documented in the form of reports or data. Lifetime employment supported this practice. At one time, Japanese companies did not have to be afraid of their employees leaving their companies and could therefore allow them to gain a high degree of company-related know-how. In many Japanese firms, knowledge is therefore communicated from person to person, and on-the-job training is preferred. Because of this, knowledge also flows freely within a Japanese firm, a fact that supported Japanese advances in new product development.

- New product development in Japan occurs in large development teams that have more autonomy than their Western counterparts. They include various members of the firm and also consumers. The development process is group-oriented—every individual idea is forwarded to the group, which then discusses and refines it until all members of the group agree on it. A strong group orientation is the reason why Japanese firms have a lower rate of radical innovations than U.S. firms. They are, however, leading when it comes to customer-oriented and high-quality products.
- Modern knowledge management approaches attempt to overcome changes in Japanese society and the increased use of modern media.

PART II

Doing Business
With the Japanese

CHAPTER 5

Entering the Japanese Market

Japan has very particular market conditions that require a deep understanding of Japanese culture and society and the strong personal commitment of a foreign investor. Japan is still considered a difficult market, and entry into the Japanese market is an expensive and time-consuming endeavor. Even if Japan is the most developed Asian country and shows very favorable market conditions, when it comes to infrastructure, the legal system, and a low business risk, Japan's unique culture and difficult language present challenges to potential investors. International business relations are so often overshadowed by misunderstandings and miscommunication. This chapter provides an overview of the particularities companies should expect when entering the Japanese market and potential solutions for overcoming these issues. Upon completion of this chapter, you should be able to accomplish the following:

- Understand the challenges of the Japanese market
- Learn about the different stages involved in entering the Japanese market
- Understand the challenges of opening a business in Japan
- Learn how to succeed in the Japanese market
- Understand a case example of a successful Western entrepreneur in Japan

Is Japan a Challenging Market?

Cultural and language barriers present a major challenge when attempting to do business in Japan. In the year 2000, a survey of 200 companies doing business in more than 30 countries found that about 64% of survey participants believed they would face greater difficulties in Japan than in other parts of the world. Only 3% of the participating companies found doing business in Japan has become easier in the past years.[1]

Better Market-Entry Conditions

Over the past decade, conditions for entering the Japanese market have greatly improved. The recession of the 1990s has changed Japan's business environment because the slow economic growth rates during that time, as well as the realization that many Japanese firms should develop more international styles of management, have led to a more positive attitude toward foreign investors and businesses entering the Japanese market. The country has therefore become a more hospitable market for foreign investors over the past years. The Japanese government, which used to protect its market quite rigidly, changed its strategy at the beginning of the 21st century and initiated a number of campaigns to attract investors to the Japanese market. The most famous one is INVEST Japan, introduced by Prime Minister Koizumi in 2003. Since then, many reforms, including the first reform of Japanese company law since the 1970s, have further eased market-entry processes. Japan has thus become an interesting place for foreign direct investment.

Advantages When Investing in Japan

Low Risk

Foreign investors frequently mention the low business risk when doing business in Japan. The payment behavior of Japanese customers is reported to be very good.[2] Interestingly, foreign investors consider it advantageous to be perceived as a *gaijin* (non-Japanese) company. While this foreignness is often viewed in the literature as a "liability" that needs to be overcome,[3] it proves to be a key advantage in the Japanese market. Managers report that it allows them to move more freely in the market and that it enables them to form strategies for differentiation from Japanese competitors.[4] With the majority (99.7%) of Japanese companies in the small- and medium-sized sectors, local competition is largely domestic-market focused and lacks effective strategies for international competition. Foreign companies that show a high degree of differentiation often manage to turn this market trend to their own advantage.[5]

Fast Break-Even Period

Also, investments in Japan appear to bear fruit fairly quickly. In a survey conducted by the German chamber of commerce, about 47% of the companies reported a break-even period of less than 4 years. About 4% of companies reported a break-even period of 10 years for their investments.[6]

Reliable Infrastructure and Legal System

In comparison to other Asian markets, Japan has the most advanced and reliable economic and legal environments. Infrastructure in Japan can be considered the best organized in the world. Trains and deliveries are always on time and performed with great care. The legal system is often considered less transparent than in the West, but it still ensures that rights and interests of foreign corporations are protected.

A Highly Developed and Wealthy Consumer Market

The major reason to invest in Japan, however, is the size and the wealth of its consumer market. Japanese consumers are not only very interested in foreign products and technology; they are also willing to pay high prices for products that meet their quality expectations.

Challenges When Investing in Japan

The main challenges when investing in Japan are cultural and linguistic differences. As one can deduce from reading this book, Japanese business practices are very unique and require a certain amount of adaptation from the investor. However, over the past several years, it has become easier to do business in Japan. Attitudes have also changed among Japanese firms and managers, and the need to internationalize and to speak English is obvious.

The following section provides some advice on which aspects to consider when entering the Japanese market. It was written by Paul Gaspari who conducted a survey among foreign entrepreneurs in Japan and investigated which aspects they find most demanding when establishing a business in Japan.

Entering the Japanese Market: The Important Rules You Should First Know

By Paul Gaspari

1. Know your new country

One of the first things that companies wanting to expand overseas, or start a business in a new country, should know is simply: where are they going? Every person is raised differently, and what seems natural to one person would never even enter the mind of someone else. When people move to a new country, it is only natural that they tend to congregate with people of similar backgrounds.

But where this becomes a problem is, if a person lives amongst this community of expatriates in a similar area, he or she never gets to the "mainland." A person can quite easily create a little island for himself in a foreign country, where he is protected from the foreign country by a sea of familiarity and new country ignorance. Japan is no exception. Entire communities of Brazilians, Filipinos, and even Americans exist in Japan where they can have little contact with the majority of the rest of the country. If you want to target people living in Japan, you should actually learn about Japan and try to get to know the country.

2. Know the laws . . . those on paper and those that are not

This is another rather simple rule of thumb. What's legal in one country, may not be legal in another. Or if it is legal, there may still be other factors in place such as customs and regulations that can make a business operation difficult. Countries also have import restrictions on certain products, which could affect the materials you need for your business. If your business aims to be in an industry with a number of laws guiding it, you need to take the time to get familiar with these laws.

At the same time, there are rules that are not "on the books" that businesses seem to learn. These local "tricks of the trade" become beneficial and may even be necessary to doing business in a foreign country. Outdated laws, stifling bureaucracy, and corrupt officials are common everywhere. I'm not advocating a policy of doing things that are illegal, but there are many shortcuts in place to avoid tedious, pointless, and time wasting government paperwork. While one can get familiar with laws and customs on the books, it takes a while to learn the perfectly legal shortcuts that they can take in their new country. Trial and error, and also networking with other expatriates, is one way to become familiar with these shortcuts.

3. Know the language . . . or at least, some of it

It seems like common sense to actually know a foreign language if you are intending on living and operating a business in a foreign country. English has slowly become the international language for business. This therefore means that for native English speakers, there are a greater number of natives that can aid and assist a business in a foreign country. Many of the foreigners who start businesses in Japan do so with a partner who is a native speaker of Japanese. This eliminates the need to know and understand a lot of the complex legal vocabulary and offers an opportunity to attract more native customers with poor English skills.

The reason I do advocate having some understanding of the foreign language is how closely language and culture are mixed. Business opportunities abound for those who can "dig deeper" into a culture, and language is usually the tool for this. Advertisements are often used to draw on some kind of shared common knowledge amongst a native population, and foreigners do not often understand the in-jokes and expressions common to their new country. By learning the foreign language, people can better understand the popular culture of their new country and use that to their advantage in business.

4. Know the people (and their tastes and customs)

Language skills need to be used to understand the people of a foreign culture, their tastes, and their preferences. As said earlier, what works in one country may not work in another country. This is all dependent on the people who live there. In all areas of a country's culture, it is the people that influence what is acceptable and normal and what is not. At the same time, regional differences exist in the peoples of different countries. Aside from language differences, certain things are more valued in regions than others.

In business the differences in tastes and an understanding of regional traditions is important to know. The business culture of a country is very important and how people behave needs to influence your own actions. In some countries, giving gifts during contract negotiations is not seen as a form of bribery but an important part of the process. Bonding over drinking with workers and clients, even if a person does not want to drink, is important for some cultures. If a country has a monarch, popular strong leader or a certain belief system, making comments and jokes about these things can be overheard and result in you being treated negatively by your hosts. In addition to these general tips, try to observe little things about what your foreign colleagues are doing. In Japan for instance, seating arrangements in cars, at restaurants, and even where to stand in elevators is carefully done according to company seniority. While a foreigner is not expected to know or abide by these customs, it does help build credibility and your commitment to a country if you understand its people and honor their customs.

5. And finally . . . know yourself!

Finally, an important thing that needs to be considered when starting your own business is your own strengths and weaknesses. People can often decide what type of business to start based on how much money they think they will make, giving little attention to the fact that they may not be right for that business. The IT and financial industries are huge money makers for many multinationals, but a single entrepreneur with no computer or financial background in these areas will probably have no chance of succeeding. If a person is good at something, and actually enjoys doing it, then what industry and country to enter should be based on that category.

Yes, opportunities are around, even if you are not an expert or a fan of a particular product or industry. But if people have a real passion for something, then they are generally motivated to learn and talk about it more. Their enthusiasm spreads to their employees, and this creates better company morale which can lead to greater sales. The energy and interest you have in the new enterprise should help sustain you during the long hours and investment you put into your company during its initial stages.

At the same time, you should also know where your own individual talents lay. You may not be a good public speaker, so you might want a partner to be the "face" of your company. You may not be good with numbers, so you would do wise to hire a diligent accountant. Try to understand your own talents and use them to your advantage while also recognizing your own weaknesses. A good manager is not someone who can do everything; it is a person that has the talent to know where to use his strengths while compensating for his weaknesses. This applies not just to his staff but also to himself as well.

Source: www.paulgaspari.com

Stages of Market Entry

Entering the Japanese market mostly follows a very typical pattern. Investors rarely enter the market without the help of a local company, and it is typical to start their first activities in the Japanese market with the help of a Japanese importer. In many cases, this trading house is a classic *sôgô shosha*, or general trading company, but increasingly, smaller companies have proven to be good partners for market entries as well. Cooperation with trading companies is especially useful since the foreign company name or brand might not be very well known in Japan.

The first step in entering the market is to import goods to Japan and to enter some retail channels. The Japanese partner can support these attempts and open up various channels for the foreign firm. Usually, this export cooperation lasts for about 5 years, a time span in which the investor gains a lot of experience in dealings with Japan. When sales increase, different ideas about product management by both the investor and the Japanese importer often become evident. At this point, many investors decide to open up their own subsidiaries[7] and manage independently in Japan. By that time, the investor has gained a substantial amount of market experience and has adapted management processes to Japanese standards.

The following section describes the challenges that Western firms meet when entering the Japanese market and explains how to successfully overcome these challenges.

Stage 1: Decision to Enter the Japanese Market

In the first stage, investors make the decision to choose the Japanese market over other potential markets. As we understand, the Japanese market not only has many advantages for foreign investors but also holds cultural and linguistic challenges. In this first market entry stage, many investors face the following problems.

Little Information on the Japanese Market

Japanese are avid collectors of information. A large amount of market and industry information is available in English and can be found via the websites of Japanese trade associations and the chambers of commerce. These institutions offer support in finding local partners, importers, or trading companies and in accessing the Japanese market. Table 5.1 provides a list of organizations that support foreign companies who plan to enter the Japanese market.

Table 5.1. Support Organizations for Entering the Japanese Market

Organization	URL	Description
Japan External Trade Organization	http://www.jetro.go.jp/ top/index.html	Affiliated with the Ministry of Economy, Trade, and Industry (METI), this pseudogovernment organization is responsible for promoting Japanese external trade and attracting foreign businesses into Japan. They have a number of programs in place to assist foreigners with starting their own businesses in Japan.
Ministry of Economy, Trade, and Industry	http://www.meti.go.jp	Japanese government industry responsible for business and industry
Delegation of the European Union to Japan	http://www.deljpn .ec.europa.eu/?ml _lang=en	Organization for EU representatives in Japan
Japan Small and Medium Enterprise Agency	http://www.chusho .meti.go.jp	Government agency that promotes SMEs in Japan
Tokyo Metropolitan Government Bureau of Industrial and Labor Affairs	http://www.tokyo -business.jp/eng/ index.html	Organization responsible for business support for foreign firms
Tokyo Chamber of Commerce and Industry	http://www.tokyo-cci .or.jp	Offers networking opportunities and business establishment support
Japan Chamber of Commerce and Industry	http://www.jcci.or.jp	Promotes international business activities
Osaka Chamber of Commerce and Industry	http://www.osaka.cci .or.jp	Supports businesses in the Kansai area (Osaka)
Nagoya Chamber of Commerce and Industry	http://www.nagoya -cci.or.jp	Support business in the Nagoya area
Small and Medium Enterprises Information of Japan	http://www.sme.ne.jp/ japane.html	Provides information on SME activities and politics in Japan
EU-Japan Center for Industrial Cooperation	http://www.eu-japan .eu/global	Organization devoted to improving business relations between the EU and Japan
European Business Council in Japan	http://www.ebc-jp .com	Organization representing the various EU chambers of commerce in Japan on trade policy and business issues

Needed Commitment Is Underestimated

The Japanese market requires a lot of dedication and personal commitment. Many companies underestimate the time and effort necessary to be successful. The manager in charge of the market entry especially has to have the patience and make the effort to build relationships with customers.

Local Marketing Research Is Expensive

Many corporations entering the Japanese market are reluctant to spend money on investigating the local market. Marketing and market research is extremely expensive. Despite this, it is advisable to obtain information on the industry of interest, on competitors, and on the newest trends. Local trade organizations and JETRO (Japan External Trade Organization) can also provide information on the Japanese market. In Table 5.2, we can see an overview of the challenges when entering the Japanese market.

Table 5.2. Challenges When Attempting to Enter the Japanese Market

Market-entry stage	Processes	Barriers	Proposed solution
Market-entry decision	Market choice	• No Japan strategy • No Asia strategy • Commitment is underestimated	Development of a long-term internationalization strategy
		Cultural distance is perceived as very high	• Conduct look-and-see trips • Search for managers with Japanese experiences
	Positioning	Local market research is difficult	Local trade commission or own market research

Stage 2: Finding and Cooperating with a Japanese Business Partner

Finding a Japanese Business Partner Is Challenging

Most Western firms begin their entry into the Japanese market by first importing their products, which helps them investigate the reaction and interest of Japanese customers. However, Japanese distribution channels are difficult to get into; a Japanese trading company is thus often the most popular way of initiating market entry.

Finding a potential Japanese business partner is the most challenging part of the market-entry processes in Japan. Most market-entry processes fail in this stage. The name and reputation of one's company, as well as one's partner, are highly important in Japan. Given that well-established company names open many doors and facilitate negotiation processes, an influential business partner can substantially ease the pains of the market-entry process. The identification of potential business partners may require some patience. Most foreign companies report that it may take up to 6 or 9 months to find an appropriate business partner.[8]

Generally, potential Japanese partners are very meticulous in accumulating detailed information above and beyond company history, business engagements outside the Japanese market, and company reputation. The diligence with which Japanese corporations pursue the process can be very irritating for foreign investors who lack Japan-specific experience, which is why investors often report this phase of market entry to be the most challenging.[9] Once a partner is found, however, the product can be easily imported to the market, and the foreign investor gets access to the distribution channel.

The First 5 Years of Cooperation

Cooperating with a Japanese business partner presents a very good opportunity for the investor to gain his first experiences working in the Japanese market, to assess market possibilities, and to start product management. The local partner supports these efforts and is mostly involved in finding suitable distribution outlets. However, in many cases, the cooperation with a Japanese partner does end after about 5 years.

Conflict With the Japanese Partner

After a few years of cooperating with the Japanese business partner, the investor has gained a lot of experience in the Japanese market and has often discovered that the market potential is greater than expected. Once a partnership is established, the Japanese partner presents and sells the product service to existing customers. But the foreign partner also expects the Japanese partner to increase the customer base. The Japanese partner, however, is very strongly involved in Japanese-style relationships and cannot simply address new customers. Another frequent point of disagreement is the brand management conducted by the Japanese partner, who, in many cases, uses price promotions to increase sales but does not professionally manage the existing product portfolio. Many investors try to solve initial disputes with the help of a mediator. The local chambers of commerce have experience in supporting conflict solutions in these cases.

However, by this point, the investor may find that the Japanese partner does not explore business opportunities to the extent that satisfies the Western headquarters, and many foreign investors begin to recognize the need for more control over management activities. At this point, the

Table 5.3. Challenges When Looking for a Business Partner in Japan

Market-entry stage	Processes	Barriers	Proposed solution
First market entry—search for business partner	Passive export	• Choice of partner often accidental • Direct search for partner is difficult	Support by local trade commissions
	Export management	• Partner also distributes rival's products • Partner addresses no new customers • Partner influences brand image and positioning	Mediation; expatriate to support marketing

investor may decide to open up a fully owned subsidiary. The possibility of ending the partnership after a certain time should therefore be clearly stated in the initial partnership agreement.

Stage 3: Opening a Business in Japan

Management Challenges

Adaptation processes prove to be very challenging for many investors since product and service adaptation not only is costly but also consumes resources and time. Furthermore, for reasons of scale and scope efficiency, Western headquarters are inherently very reluctant to allow a nonstandard-ized marketing mix. Foreign managers report that this standardization-versus-adaptation aspect provides a strong potential for conflicts between headquarters and local representatives.

Choosing and Finding a Local CEO

One of the first issues to arise in developing a Japanese subsidiary is whether to hire a Japanese or Western manager. Many investors prefer to hire an expatriate to manage their subsidiary in order to establish a high level of control and reduce communication difficulties. When dealing with traditional industries (e.g., construction) or a large number of small and medium-sized enterprises, hiring a Japanese manager with industry experience may be most useful. Most business partners in these industries do not speak English and may feel intimidated when negotiating with

Table 5.4. Challenges When Establishing a Subsidiary in Japan

Market-entry stage	Barriers	Proposed solution
Establishment of Japanese business	Finding a local CEO	Expatriates with Japanese experience and Japanese language skills
	Building contacts takes a number of years	Network the "Japanese way"
	Gaining customer trust in non-Japanese products and company is difficult	Long-term customer relationships needed

their non-Japanese counterparts. In younger industries, or when cooperating with business partners in Tokyo, foreign managers have become commonplace, and they have been very successful. In any event, a manager of a Japanese subsidiary should also have several years of experience in the Japanese market and, if possible, should speak Japanese well. Hiring an expatriate to manage the subsidiary has a number of advantages for the foreign investor. A non-Japanese manager can act more freely and also apply business strategies that may not be very popular in Japan. It is also often easier for foreigners to address new customers—Japanese businesspeople are not at ease addressing customers who are not acquainted with their company and tend to depend on hierarchies and already-existing company relationships. Female foreign managers report little hindrances when working in Japan. Since business in Japan is dominated by men, foreign women stick out in any industry as something special and find it, in many cases, a lot easier to talk to customers and establish relationships with clients or other industry members.[10]

Finding and Keeping Japanese Staff

Abbeglen and Stalk[11] reported that Western companies setting up for the Japanese market had problems finding qualified staff. Japanese companies traditionally hire employees right after their graduation and provide lifelong employment, a seniority promotion system, and an array of "typical" flexible fringe benefits (e.g., bonus payments). Emotional bonds with the company are therefore very high, and there has been a great reluctance by Japanese employees to change jobs during their careers. Working for a foreign company is typically considered a risk since lifetime employment is not guaranteed and return to a "traditional" Japanese company would be impossible. Western or foreign firms, especially those that do not have a widely recognized brand name, face a dilemma in hiring qualified employees in Japan. Male university graduates strive for jobs in big Japanese firms where they will be trained by the company and have a lifetime secured job. They can only be recruited with great difficulty. Young Japanese women, even if well educated and ambitious, have little chance of building a successful career in a Japanese firm (see chapter 7). Even if they are able to enter a prestigious firm, they often do not get the chance to climb up the corporate ladder and have a family at the same time. For many women, these conditions leave them with only one option: to work in a foreign company in Japan. So foreign firms only have the choice of Japanese males who cannot, or do not want to, enter a prestigious Japanese firm or female applicants who cannot enter them because of male prejudice. This competition is usually won by the qualified females, and Western firms are especially well known for hiring more women in Japan than they often would in their home countries.[12]

Due to the economic crisis of 2008 and the increasingly insecure job market in Japan, working conditions within foreign enterprises in Japan—such as greater workforce diversity, Western holiday systems, and other features—are becoming more and more appreciated by Japanese employees, men and women alike.

Succeeding in the Japanese Market

A major necessity when doing business with the Japanese is a high degree of adaptation to Japanese consumers and market processes. Japan is one of the most sophisticated markets in the world and cannot be compared to other Asian markets. Japanese consumers are accustomed to high service levels and product quality. Japanese tastes and interests often differ from Western ones. It is therefore often difficult to transfer Western marketing concepts to the Japanese market. This may be one of the biggest obstacles in entering the Japanese market—many companies that have been successful in other parts of the world have stumbled badly in Japan.[13]

Higher Expectations Toward Foreign Corporations

Foreign companies are confronted with high expectations, requirements, and demands of Japanese consumers, who generally assume that the quality of Japanese products is higher than that of Western products, and they are willing to pay higher prices for them, too. Japanese consumers and customers also require extensive information about the product and the company. Since they show a higher trust toward companies with a long history and a good reputation, it is very important to provide information on the company history. Many investors therefore provide a great amount of information about the company itself in the form of detailed pamphlets written in Japanese. Distributing product information in English is not advisable.

Another important aspect when selling consumer products is packaging. The packaging of a product, especially if it is a present, is a means for showing courtesy and respect. Most producers are required to develop special packages and wrapping to meet Japanese consumer tastes.

Building Long-Lasting Relationships

Doing business with the Japanese is strongly based on interpersonal relationships. These relationships develop over a long period of time. The Japanese prefer partners they trust. Developing this trust is accomplished through a number of personal meetings. One short visit or contacts made at one trade fair are usually not sufficient for building a long-lasting, profitable business relationship. One of the most important factors is the time spent with the customer—the longer, the better. Dealing with customers in Japan therefore means spending a lot of time with them and possibly also spending some money entertaining them. The more time that is spent with a potential client, the more there is interest and commitment shown in return.

Be Patient and Stick With It!

Success does not always come the first time in a venture. Often, it takes several tries and several ideas before a person becomes a successful business owner. But foreigners do not have the same social pressures for success as the Japanese. They can fail in this market and try again. They learn from their mistakes and can improve on their weaknesses. By being patient with the market, really trying to understand it, and learning what works and what does not, a foreigner can ultimately find a niche there and create his or her own successful enterprise.[14]

Being a Foreign Entrepreneur in Japan

An increasing number of non-Japanese become entrepreneurs in Japan. They take advantage of the profitability of the Japanese market or sell products to the growing expatriate community in Japan. The Japanese

Table 5.5. Overview of Challenges When Entering the Japanese Market

Market-entry stage	Barriers	Proposed solution
Market establishment	Intercultural management within Japanese subsidiary	Intercultural training
	Japanese customer service	Japanese sales personnel
	Development of long-term and midterm market goals	Market and competition need to be researched by Japanese staff
	Finding Japanese employees	Hire female Japanese managers
	Product quality must be adapted (in almost every case)	Regard Japan as benchmark for all business processes
Meeting Japanese expectations	Higher service level	Japanese service personnel
	Constant demand for innovative products	Product screening in headquarters
	Product packaging needs to be improved (except for import products)	Develop packaging for Japanese market
	Long memory for product defects	One or two extra tests for every product imported

government supports entrepreneurs regardless of nationality. The new Japanese company law has improved and has eased conditions under which a business can be established.

Many local communities provide special assistance to Western companies planning to establish a business, such as free office space and consulting. Kanazawa prefecture, which is next to Tokyo, has become a very attractive place for investors. JETRO offers numerous answers to frequently asked questions on the topic, best practices cases, and free consulting and business-partner matching services on their website (www .jetro.org).

The following section describes the experiences of an entrepreneur from New Zealand who established a successful travel business in Japan.

Starting a Travel Agency in Japan

By Gina Whittle, CEO and Founder of
New Zealand Life Tours, Fukuoka, Japan

Initially I chose Japan because I was interested in the language and was already here studying. I wanted to stay here longer and did research into finding an industry or business that I could start. This happened to be a New Zealand specific education & travel agency, a niche which was yet unfilled in Japan. Having said that establishing and running a business is a lot cheaper in Fukuoka, a town in Southern Japan, hence you can test the market before moving on to the larger cities of Osaka or Tokyo. Being in a provincial city, rather than Tokyo, the main obstacles were not having any other business owners who had succeeded here. Hence it was often difficult for Japanese companies to deal with a foreign owner. I believe this is a particular Japanese trait that the trust must be built up over years before business can take place.

Opening a business is supported by an efficient administration and infrastructure. The benefits of having a business in Japan are the flexibility and independence. The tax regime in Japan is also very favorable, as are low interest rates for business loans. The living standard in Japan is very high and the convenience of the transportation systems, internet etc. means that everything is at your fingertips and you can achieve a lot in one working day. The huge population in Japan means the labor force is fantastic. Staffs are very loyal and have strong work ethics.

However, Japan is a challenging market. The expectations of customers in Japan are very high. You have to study the culture and customers and deliver a product that has the quality people request. Over recent years however customers have become more price conscious, but still expect very high quality. This can be a challenge at times.

Many people think that being a foreigner in Japan would be a disadvantage in establishing a company, however from my experience it has been my greatest advantage. Being a Westerner, you are more independent compared to a Japanese manager, who would be expected to do a lot more in the community. People are interested in what I'm doing and I have received a great amount of support from the local community. As for a foreigner in Japan people don't expect you to know everything and in fact, this makes them more patient and willing to explain business procedures. Being a Westerner you stand out compared to a Japanese manager which gives your company a uniqueness and marketing advantage. Having experience of Western marketing strategies or ways of doing business is a huge advantage as most companies are often quite conservative and conventional in their way of doing things. Hence it's quite easy to stand apart from your competition.

Also being in Fukuoka again, there are very few English speakers so everything had to be in Japanese. In my experience, being a foreigner doesn't mean you should neglect mastering the language. Some foreigners think it is fine to conduct business in Japan without knowing much of the language and instead rely on interpreters. I wouldn't recommend this. I think if you can't communicate directly with your business counterpart it's difficult to establish a strong rapport and especially in Japan trust and mutual understanding is the key to establishing successful relationships. Whilst I initially had some difficulties with communicating in Japanese, I've worked hard to gain more language skills, study the Japanese system of business and create strong networks with Japanese businesspeople. Because of this I now feel a great part of the local community and can call Fukuoka home. For someone thinking of starting a company in Japan I highly recommend learning the language. Also having one Japanese person in the company who understands Western ways can help bridge the gap between the Western and Japanese mindset. Social networking is also essential, and compared to Western countries this often means business dinners on evenings and weekends.

Learning the language certainly isn't the only challenge. Initially, I was told by several Japanese and foreign businesspeople that it is impossible for a foreigner to loan money for a business without a Japanese guarantor. Well after hearing this several times it made me even more determined to try and apply for a business loan. I applied once and it was denied, and 6 months later I tried again and my application was accepted. This process taught me a great lesson that persistence really does pay-off, especially as a foreigner.

Japan doesn't happen overnight, it has to be a long term strategy. But once you develop a business relationship with someone in Japan it is there to stay.

Source: http://www.nzlifetours.com

Summary

- The Japanese market is generally seen as a competitive and culturally challenging market. Over the past several years, attitudes of Japanese government and businesses toward foreign investment have improved and have made market entry easier. The Japanese market is the world's second-largest consumer market, and it offers low business risk, a fast break-even period in most cases, a well-organized and reliable infrastructure and legal system, and high profit margins.
- When deciding to enter the Japanese market, corporations often underestimate the commitment needed for Japan and have difficulty finding adequate information in English.
- When attempting to find a Japanese business partner, cross-cultural misunderstandings often present a major challenge. Most market entries fail in this stage.
- After a period of 3 to 5 years in the Japanese market, many investors decide to open up their own businesses. Challenges in this stage include finding the right staff and CEO for the local firm, adapting quality standards to Japanese consumer expectations, and building long-lasting relationships with Japanese business partners.

CHAPTER 6

Succeeding as a Foreign Manager in a Japanese Firm

Managing in a Japanese firm can be very challenging for non-Japanese. Even today, while Japanese business practices are changing, tradition and Japan's unique culture play a major role when working in Japan. The complex Japanese language and traditional business practices, such as seniority principles, present hurdles to Western managers in Japan. Project management and strategic goal development also greatly differ from the West, and non-Japanese managers working in Japan are urged to adapt their managing style and attitudes. This chapter explores the most popular Japanese business practices. Upon completion of this chapter, you should be able to understand the following:

- What the different levels of Japanese language are and how they are used
- What the main aspects of Japanese communication are
- How to lead and motivate a Japanese team
- What a *ringi-sho* is and how it is used in the Japanese firm
- What *nemawashi* is and how you can use it to achieve your goals
- How Japanese strategic management differs from the West
- What to consider when managing a Japanese project

Communication Within the Japanese Firm

Japanese Language (Nihongo)

The most obvious obstacle for non-Japanese managers is the Japanese language—*Nihongo*. The Japanese language is, without doubt, one of the most complicated languages. It takes a minimum of 2 or 3 years of intensive study to master this language at a conversation level, and there are "few Westerners who have systematically learned both—realistically, doing so requires a university-level intensity of study."[1] The writing system consists of three different character sets: *kanji* (several thousands of Chinese characters) and *hiragana* and *katakana* (two syllabaries of 46 characters each, together called *kana*). Japanese texts can be written in two ways: in Western style, horizontally from top to bottom, or in traditional Japanese style, vertically from right to left. Both writing styles exist side-by-side today.

Honorific Language (Keigo)

There are three basic levels of Japanese language: the "low" level, used when addressing subordinates; the "intimate" level, used when conversing with family members and close friends of the same age; and an "honorific" level (*keigo*), used when addressing superiors and respected elders.[2] Essentially, *keigo* refers to the distinctive style of speech or writing used to show respect to persons and sometimes to sacred things such as shrines or temples. For instance, there are more than five different words for the English word "you," each of which is used depending on whom the speaker is talking to. In formal situations and in business negotiations, an honorific language level (*keigo*) is used.

Keigo can be broken down into three separate categories: *sonkeigo*, respectful or honorific language; *kenjogo*, humble language; and *teineigo*, polite language. *Sonkeigo* is used when addressing or speaking about a person of higher status; in this case, honorific vocabulary is used to show politeness. *Kenjogo* is used when speaking about oneself (or one's company) to a person of higher rank. Here, the speaker uses humble and modest words to show respect. *Teineigo* is the term for generally speaking politely. Foreigners are often advised to use *teineigo* because it is easier to use than the two other forms.

Communication Styles

High-Context Communication

Based on the idea of keeping harmony, communication in Japan is often indirect. Hall and Hall[3] define this as high-context communication.

Every message communicated by a Japanese person is surrounded by a context, which needs to be understood by the person who is spoken to. If a Japanese person, for example, says "maybe," he or she is saying an honorific "no" in a less direct manner. When speaking to a Westerner, who assumes that the word "maybe" refers to the possibility that an event might take place, this can lead to great misunderstandings.

The Japanese communication style is therefore considered to be highly dependent on context:[4] every message is surrounded by some unspoken information that both communicators are supposed to understand. The message can only be correctly understood if both communicators share a context and know or sense what the other person intends to say. Western communication, on the contrary, is considered low context, as the message content is the exact message and there is no invisible message beyond the words exchanged. "No" means just "no," and "maybe" means there is a 50% chance of things happening.

Reading the Air (Kuki o Yomu)

The context in which messages and information are exchanged is extremely important in Japan, and from an early age, Japanese people learn to read the context surrounding a message or to interpret the atmosphere of a conversation.

High-context orientation and a need to respect other people's feelings lead to a great sensitivity for feelings and intentions, even if they are not explicitly stated. The Japanese call this "reading the air" (*kuki o yomu*). A person who can read the air understands things without being told and can sense if a friend or colleague is angry or stressed. Being able to "read the air" is a virtue in Japanese society. The Japanese often expect Westerners to be able to do this, too, but most Westerners find it easier to understand other people's feelings if they are expressed in words. The directness involved in this is often considered rude in Japan and can lead to cross-cultural conflict.

Private and Public Opinion (Honne and Tatemae)

The Japanese differentiate between public and private life and also between their "public" (*tatemae*) and "private" (*honne*) opinions. *Honne* can be translated as the private opinion and *tatemae* as the public opinion. In business, *tatemae* is a must during negotiations or on other official occasions. This means that people (businessmen or others) will express an opinion that is expected from them even if this is not what they really think or consider correct. *Honne*, on the other hand, expresses the speaker's real and "honest" opinion, which may not always be expressed in public or in the corporate environment.

Honne and *tatemae* are present in all contexts of modern Japanese life and are probably the two concepts that are most difficult to understand for Westerners. Foreigners often perceive Japanese communication styles as vague and as avoiding straight business talk. Practically, a suitable approach in tackling the difficulties in communicating with the Japanese is to ask many polite and indirect questions. This may help to develop a better sense of a counterpart's true opinion.[5]

Participative Leadership

Japanese leadership style revolves around participation. Japanese team leaders or CEOs have a more coordinating role than their Western counterparts, who are expected to bring in individual ideas and, sometimes, to turn the company around. Japanese leadership, on the other hand, mainly aims to coordinate opinions and intentions of team members and help group-oriented decision-making processes to run smoothly. This management style is based on the idea that one person alone cannot be cleverer than all members of a team combined. Assertive leadership can therefore hardly be expected.

In the West, one person can take individual responsibility for a company decision even if this decision affects the lives of thousands of other employees. In Japan, this is not the case; here, leadership is group oriented and people believe that it is too risky to let only one person decide over many others. All decisions have to be approved by other board members, and in many cases, the CEO or president is more of a coordinator than a decision maker. In recent years, there have been changes at companies like UNIQLO, where the CEO is also the founder and the owner of the firm, but in traditional firms such as Toyota, there was no strong leader figure in the past decade.

Motivation and Involvement

Working hard and not giving up until a goal is achieved are considered the highest virtues in Japan. All group members in a Japanese group are expected to form a strong, harmonious unit; to perform according to the rules; and to stick to processes. The overall well-being of the group is the most important goal, and all team members are dedicated to this. Next to performing tasks in the best possible way, achievement orientation plays another major role in Japanese society and management.

Doing One's Best (Ganbaru)

There are two main concepts of achievement orientation that can be observed almost everywhere in Japan. The most important concept is *ganbaru*. *Ganbaru* translates as doing one's best or never giving up, but it is a bit more involved than this. It also means to finish a task and to never stop until a goal is achieved. *Ganbaru* is an active process, meaning that one has to try as hard as possible to reach a certain goal. There are many hurdles and examinations in every Japanese person's life, and to try to overcome these obstacles (even if not successful) is a most important task. People following *ganbaru* try to achieve a goal or fulfill a difficult task even if it might be very painful. In Japanese society it is considered a weakness to give up a plan or to look for an easier option. Trying as hard as one can (e.g., working very hard to get into a good company or university) is seen as a virtue.

Endurance (Gaman)

The second concept that is worth discussing is *gaman*. *Gaman* refers to the ability to withstand and bear something unpleasant that cannot be changed right away and that one has no control over. Going to work on a very crowded Tokyo train during rush hour is a situation where people usually *gaman*. But *gaman* can also be seen at the workplace, where people keep working even if they would rather not stay as long as their boss.

Ganbaru and *gaman* differ from each other. Where *ganbaru* is an active process and requires people to do something to achieve their goals, *gaman* is passive and focuses more on enduring and not complaining.

However, both concepts are the major reason for Japan's successful development after World War II. Even today, working hard and trying one's best are viewed as good attributes, and a good employee is a person who is trying to dedicate as much time and energy to the firm as possible. *Ganbaru* is the reason for the unbelievable motivation that many Japanese show when it comes to work.

Involvement With the Firm and Dedication to Work (Marugakae)

Even today, Japanese employees exhibit very high motivation when working and dedicate themselves to their company. Traditionally, *salarymen* had very little time for their families because they were even expected to spend part of their free time in the company or with their colleagues. This attitude is also the reason for long working hours and the low number of holidays. The term *marugakae* refers to the state of being absorbed in one's company, resulting in a total dedication of the employee to the company. Marugakae can also be translated as completely financed, sponsored, or under patronage. In ancient Japan, marugakae was an expected attitude for personal servants in their relationships to landlords. The concept of marugakae stands for the employee's identification, loyalty, and emotional bond with the company, with little separation between private and professional life in Japan.

But dedicating one's life to the company also had negative effects on the Japanese society. Marugakae is often executed to an excessive level and harms the health of not only many Japanese employees but also their families. Long work hours are still common in Japan. A phenomenon often discussed is *karoshi*, or death by overworking, which became a synonym for the Japanese working style. The two main causes of *karoshi* are heart attack or stroke due to stress and fatigue from long hours in the office. Moreover, there are cases where work-related problems have created personal problems for employees, leading them to commit suicide.

Risk Avoidance

High involvement in the group and a shared responsibility for each member further leads to a tendency to avoid risk and to ensure that all team

Motivating a Japanese Team

- Always communicate the overall group goal and stress each team member's responsibility for reaching the group goal. Individual goals do not motivate Japanese employees very much!
- Make room in your work schedule for social gatherings such as team dinners, karaoke parties, or an eventual tea break. The Japanese feel more motivated if they have a personal relationship with all team members.
- Rewards should be team rewards and not stress competition among team members. For big ambitious projects, Japanese companies often sponsor team travel or an overnight trip to an *onsen* (hot spring resort) for their employees.
- Actively show that you are a member of the team. In Japan, team leaders have fatherlike roles and take care of their employees.
- Take the time to explain expectations and processes very clearly to all team members. Big team meetings are better than small ones for getting all team members on the same page.
- Work harder than the rest. Since you are considered the most influential and powerful person in the group, you have to show more dedication and motivation than your team members.

members are safe. Japanese organizations and teams therefore try to make decisions that benefit all members of the group, making sure that no one is left out. Group decision making is one way of achieving this; another is to share responsibility within a team. In comparison to Western leaders, Japanese managers have less individual power and always have to include the opinions of other members of the board. In most cases, risk is shared among all group members; one person or manager will hardly ever be seen as responsible for a project or a result. This leads to long discussion processes in which all aspects of a problem are discussed and relationships are taken care of. In times of crisis, Japanese corporations therefore find it very difficult to act quickly and to find radical solutions for existing problems.

Risk avoidance also leads to a high degree of discipline, which is evident to even cursory visitors of Japan. In terms of business relationships, it is important to realize that overly careful planning is necessary for preparing negotiations and meetings between potential partners.

Group Decision Making

In the West, top managers have a more powerful role than they do in Japan. Leadership is more individual oriented, and a leader can make decisions for other members of a group (i.e., top-down decision making). In Japan, however, a company wants to maintain harmony within the group, and decision making includes many participants and also originates at lower management levels (i.e., bottom-up decision making). This does not mean that employees refuse orders or refuse to show higher managers respect. But when it comes to finding solutions, the idea is, again, that one person can never be cleverer than all members of the group together. Another reason for a preference for group over individual decision making is the idea that all members should more or less agree on a solution or plan and should understand it very well from the beginning. The actual implementation of the decided plan or change can be carried out much faster if all people concerned agree to it and are informed about it. Team members can therefore maintain a harmonious and future-oriented relationship. Accordingly, no person alone has the authority to make decisions on an individual basis.[6]

Involving a high number of participants in the process naturally leads to a higher number of meetings, which are a characteristic of Japanese management, and these meetings often lead to a tiring and time-consuming process until a final decision is made. In case some unexpected situations turn up, the Japanese need time to adjust and find solutions that are supported by all members of their group. Work is performed such that the whole team receives praise.

Nemawashi

Generally, it is preferred that problems or unexpectancies are solved beforehand in a process called *nemawashi*. Nemawashi refers to communication between negotiators before an official meeting takes place.

Nemawashi describes a communication technique used to avoid conflicts and achieve a consensus in decision making. It describes maneuvering behind the scenes, reaching an understanding, and obtaining certain objectives.[7]

Nemawashi is usually conducted through preliminary meetings and confidential one-to-one consultations. It is supposed to prevent blindsiding or surprises and to preserve relationships and "save face."[8] In a company, this means that if a change or new idea should be promoted, it is advisable to spend a lot of time with different colleagues to warm them up to new ideas. This can be done in the form of a classic *nomikai* dinner or simply over a cup of tea.

During nemawashi, all relevant persons (groups or companies) are asked about their thoughts on the topic being discussed. They are asked to support the change or topic and are also expected to give feedback. If someone is not willing to join the consensus, he might receive soft pressure from the group. This allows all participants of a negotiation to provide feedback on ideas and circulate them among all participants. In this way, problems can be solved before a final meeting, and harmony and understanding is secured for all participants. Nemawashi is the reason why Japanese meetings often consist only of an information-exchange function and simply finalize the results of the nemawashi process.

The actual meeting should present no surprises and may be used only to discuss the results of prior discussions. *Nemawashi* is also the reason why the Japanese often cannot come to a solution or conclusion when negotiating with a foreign business partner.

The Ringi System (Ringi-Seido)

The *ringi* system is the formalized version of a group decision-making process. The main idea of the ringi system is to include and integrate ideas and suggestions of all staff members concerning new ideas, with the overall goal of gaining consensus and including the creativity and expertise of each member. By including many members of the firm, lower and middle management and their knowledge on the topic or task can also be involved.

The ringi process starts with a written proposal at the lower levels, as opposed to the upper levels, of management. An idea or proposal is first conceived by one or more members of the lower management section and is usually discussed among coworkers. Permission from higher superiors is required to actually begin the ringi process. In a ringi document (*ringi-sho*), a new idea is presented and then improved and revised by all managers involved. The document is often circulated a number of times throughout a company. The whole process is finalized once all participants agree on a solution and sign the document. The ringi-sho must then pass through each lower level sector and receive approval from most, if not all, other coworkers before being sent to the immediate superior. It can sometimes be signed by 30 or more people. Their superior will then decide whether or not to accept the proposal by either sending it to the next sector of management as a form of approval or sending it back to the coworkers for further adjustments. This process will continue until the proposal, including any and all adjustments that were made, finally reaches the top, where the head executives will either give their blessings or decide that it needs further work.

Strengths and Weaknesses of the Ringi System

The responsibility for a project lies with all levels of management, as a plan or proposal must pass through each level as it works its way up for the top brass to review. This method thus involves as many employees as possible in the decision-making process. The ringi system decreases individual responsibility and informs employees of new strategies or ideas. This allows Japanese teams, departments, and companies to set very ambitious goals, but it also involves time-consuming decision-making processes and indecisiveness in times of crisis. All members are informed and support an idea. But the *ringi* process takes time. Involving so many people in a decision-making process can mean long hours to come to conclusions.

Strategic Management

Focus on Process Orientation

Japanese management has a very strong process orientation. When working or living in Japan, this becomes evident very quickly. The strong concentration on performing even the smallest operation with great perfection has a lot of advantages and can be seen as a strong point of Japanese management. At the same time, it also leads to inflexibility and leaves the question of how Japanese management deals with strategic issues. In general, strategic management in Japan differs greatly from the West.

Following the Crowds

Whereas Western strategic management mainly focuses on being different from others, differentiating a product, or focusing on innovation and novelty, Japanese companies do not always feel the urge to reinvent the wheel. In many cases, they are very content to adapt ideas and strategies shown to be successful at other firms or in other countries. *Iitoko dori* is the term for adopting ideas, picking the best parts of them, and then Japanizing them successfully.

Other reasons for this approach include an aversion to high risk, which can be observed in most Japanese companies, and a more positive attitude toward copying other people's ideas. While copying or adapting others' ideas may be viewed as a lack of individuality or even a weakness in the West, in Asia, it is not. It is a risk-free way of achieving success.

Less Specific Goals Than in the West

Western strategic management not only differs in its orientation from Japanese strategies; strategic management in a Western firm focuses on an object or goal that is very clearly measurable, has a time frame, and is in fact achievable. Once the goal has been defined, strategies are developed and evaluated, and the best strategy is chosen. After this, plans are developed in order to put the strategy into practice. In Japan, these processes look similar but are still quite different. First of all, the goals are not defined as precisely as in the West. Whereas in the West, goals are very specific and measurable, in Japan, the goals are less clearly defined and not as specific.

Dealing With Failure

The main difference in strategic management between the East and West can be found once a strategy proves unsuccessful. In the West, unsuccessful strategies are dropped very easily. If "strategy A" does not work, one can move on to "strategy B." Shifts like this are possible and are even considered good and effective, especially if an original strategy is considered unprofitable. In Japan, this is not possible. Giving up a strategy and moving on to a new one is not acceptable. Instead, "strategy A" is molded and becomes strategy "AB" or "A*" and will be adapted until the overall strategic goal is met. The idea of simply giving up an agreed-upon plan and moving on to a new one is not at all appealing within the Japanese business environment. This can be attributed partly to the *ganbaru* attitude and partly to the fact that giving up is seen as a major weakness. Typically, because so many stakeholders are involved in developing a strategy, it cannot be simply abandoned.

Specific things to remember when developing strategies with Japanese include the following:

- Goals are more broadly defined than in the West.
- "Strategy A" cannot be abandoned, and a "plan B" is not very appreciated, either.
- There is absolutely no problem with adapting an existing strategy to fit changing requirements.
- All changes must be communicated to all team members.
- All strategies must be brought to an end (following the ganbaru attitude).

Project Management

Project management in Japan reflects all cultural aspects of Japanese management. Japanese project teams are often very large, and many team members have specific tasks to fulfill. Relationships, hierarchy, and group consensus also play important roles. The project team is a unit and not a mix of strong individuals. Japanese team members do not expect their

Table 6.1. Differences Between Japanese and Western Project Management[9]

Japanese project management	Western project management
Project organization	
• Relationship- and *nemawashi*-based organization • Individual needs and expectations of project team members are not taken care of • A high number of team members	• Project-plan-based organization • Individual needs and expectations of project team members must be taken care of • A small number of team members fulfill very different tasks
Project communication	
• Reports (weekly and monthly) play a major role • Polite speech (*keigo*) in e-mails and letters • The status of the project is explained in great detail	• Video and telephone conferences • Short, often direct messages in e-mail and fast responses • Overview of project status is given
Expectations	
• Long work hours • Orders from superiors are obeyed without questioning • Long-term perspective	• Work ends at 5:00 p.m. (and can be continued at home if necessary) • Opinions of all team members are exchanged (and may be questioned) • Short-term perspective

individual wishes and preferences to be taken care of. The group goal and the project always dominate the work.

Project communication is a major part of project organization in Japan. Weekly and monthly reports are a must, as all team members are constantly informed about all details of the progress and its status. Communication manners are polite and very strongly reflect hierarchy.

Work attitudes in Japanese project management also differ from the West. Long working hours are a standard. Japanese employees will not leave work and then continue a task at home after dinner. Within a project team, there is a clear hierarchy as in every Japanese team. Table 6.1 provides an overview of Japanese and Western project management styles.

Summary

- Japanese language is a major hurdle when managing in Japan as a foreigner. It has one of the most complicated writing systems in the world and can only be learned via an intensive university language class. The Japanese term *keigo* broadly refers to the honorific way of speaking in the Japanese language. The level of politeness has to be adapted to the person being spoken to.
- The Japanese communication style differs greatly from the West. It is highly dependent on context, and each message is surrounded by a meaning that is not explicitly communicated but is known to Japanese communicators. Western communication styles, however, mostly rely on the message itself, without taking its context into account. The Japanese are also more sensitive to unspoken messages and hints and can "read the air" of a situation much better than Western managers.

  Japanese distinguish between private and public opinions. A private opinion (*honne*) cannot always be expressed freely, for example, if it damages the overall well-being of the organization or team or in case it is considered inappropriate. In cases like this, *tatemae*, or the public opinion, is used, which generally expresses the organization's or team's attitudes.
- When managing in Japan, participative leadership is more advisable than the Western style of individual leadership. Participative leaders coordinate their team members' ideas and attitudes in developing a consensus instead of imprinting their own style onto the firm's future strategy.
- Decision-making processes in Japan are always group processes. All team members should be included in a decision. Including all members in a discussion is often called *nemawashi*, which means that all team members are warmed up to an idea before a major decision is made. Another Japanese decision-making tool is the ring*i* system. *Ringi-seido* refers to a system in which all members of a team are included in a final decision. A document (*ringi-sho*) is passed around and all participants can add their comments or suggestions in order to help improve it.

- Strategic management styles in Japan also differ from the West. In general, Japanese management is very process oriented but is often said to lack strategic skills. Many typical Japanese work attitudes are reflected in project management. Japanese project teams consist of many team members, all of whom obey all rules of Japanese interaction. There are weekly and monthly reports that update everyone involved. Teams are hierarchically structured, and rules and orders from superiors are followed without question.

CHAPTER 7

Intercultural Challenges When Working in Japan

When attempting to be successful in Japan, an understanding of the Japanese culture, society, and business etiquette is necessary. In international management, working and succeeding in Japan is often considered the most challenging thing to do. The reason why Japan is often considered in the top league of international business is not so much a challenging infrastructure or a weak legal system, as in many other Asian economies, but the strong differences in culture, which reflect on all aspects of management, as well as the Japanese language. Western managers often find the differences in working styles and problem solving especially difficult. This chapter deals with intercultural challenges that non-Japanese managers face when managing in a Japanese firm or leading a Japanese team. Upon completion of this chapter you should be familiar with the following:

- What major intercultural challenges are encountered when managing in Japan
- How Western women can succeed in the Japanese business environment

English Is Not a Global Language—At Least Not in Japan

Many Western executives expect their Japanese business partners or employees to speak English. This is not always the case. The language barrier can be a serious issue since Japanese is not a language to be learned in one or two private lessons a week. Many firms offer classes for their overseas employees, but these classes, unless they are held on a university level, will only allow participants to find their way around Tokyo or to order a drink at a bar. To be able to fluently and effectively communicate with a client, 3 to 5 years of intensive Japanese classes are necessary. It is, however, still advisable to take lessons because it will make life in Japan easier. Outside the firm, the situation is often similar: The level of spoken English is very low.

Naturally, many Western firms in Japan have bilingual staff, but in most companies, there are only a handful of them. Foreign language skills are still not a requirement for new recruits, and the majority of employees in a Japanese subsidiary usually do not speak English fluently. Even if they have studied English for many years, they may be reluctant to use it because they fear that their language skills may not be sufficient.

In case the reluctance to speak English becomes a problem, it helps to stress that language skills are not a main issue. I, for example, tell people that I am not a native speaker myself and that mistakes are no problem. These aspects should be stressed at the beginning of a meeting to make all participants more comfortable and relaxed.

Group Responsibility

In a Western firm, employees feel motivated to take on personal responsibility and individually manage a task. In Japan, this is quite the contrary. Most Japanese employees (unless they have worked for a while in a Western country) still prefer group responsibility.

Similar to most Asian societies, Japan is a group-oriented society. Any individual within a group is more likely to accept a compromise or accept the overall group opinion rather than insisting on one's own preferences and well-being. The overall belief is that a group is stronger than an individual and that tasks can be more easily achieved in a group rather than individually.

The concept of collectivism has different meanings in the East and West. Western societies are considered individual societies and are accepting when group members place their own opinions, decisions, and benefits over the benefit of other group members. From a Western perspective, collectivism and groupism are often perceived as more negative than individualism.[1] The idea of leaving a decision to a group or a group deciding over one's fate or future seems frightening. Collectivistic cultures are therefore often seen as cultures where personal freedom is limited, individual actions are controlled, and power abuse may occur.

The Asian attitude toward groups is naturally different. Being a member of a team or organization is always better than being alone. Groups and groupism are not seen as oppressive or as limiting personal freedom. Group membership comes with protection and support and allows all members to achieve greater things than they would on their own. Many Japanese perceive being in a team as relaxing. It is a frequent misunderstanding of Western managers that most Japanese would prefer more individualism (if they had the choice). But in reality, this is not always the case. Most Japanese do not find individual responsibility as pleasing as Westerners do; in many cases, it can be stressful for them because they have never experienced how to deal with this type of responsibility. On the contrary, it would stress most Western managers if they were told to simply accept decisions made by other team members and to assume that this decision was in their best interest.

So when hiring Japanese managers, note that they often prefer a group-oriented decision-making process, even if they are professionals who have extensive experience in their fields. Many of them are not comfortable managing "Western style." The following example shows a typical situation in a Western firm in Japan hiring a Japanese human resources specialist.

Culture Shock in a Western Firm

After working for more than 10 years for a Japanese corporation, Kazuo decided to accept the offer of a European manufacturer. At his former company, Kazuo was first working in different departments but had spent the last 5 years in the human resources department. He was in charge of recruiting new employees directly from Japanese universities for his corporation.

In his new job, the pay was higher and the position sounded very attractive. The European manufacturer planned to expand its business in Japan and intended to set up a brand-new recruiting and human resources department. Kazuo's position would be the new head of this department. His task was to create the new department, recruit other human resources specialists, and take responsibility for all human resources activities in the company. This all sounded really exciting, and Kazuo was very eager to accept the position.

Kazuo therefore started the new job with a lot of enthusiasm. In starting work, however, things were very different from what he expected. Instead of receiving direct instructions, he was mostly left alone in his office to perform his tasks independently. There was not much communication with his colleagues. Everybody seemed to mind his or her own business. In meetings, he was often asked about his plans and goals, and he found it very irritating that he had nobody to share his responsibilities with. During the first few months, he felt very lonely and disoriented in his new job.

In this example, the Japanese manager expected to have more freedom and a more creative job in the Western firm, but he was not familiar with taking on the whole responsibility. He was irritated and uncomfortable and tried to seek advice from his colleagues. In this case, it is advisable to support the employee in fulfilling his task. Guidance and patience are needed to explain expectations carefully and to ensure that the tasks can be performed individually. This may take a few months and cannot be expected right from the day of hiring.

Group Decision Making

The preference of slow change goes hand-in-hand with slow and group-oriented decision making, which has many benefits in times of stability and economic growth but endangers the Japanese firm in times of crisis. Japanese business and management practices are group oriented, as the organization or team as a whole is more important than each individual. The strong process orientation and group orientation, however, can become a problem in times of crisis because there is usually no "strong leader" who can push a radical change within a Japanese firm. All decisions have to be made in a group, and this takes time. Often, Japanese group decisions are very cautious and tend to play for time. The West would refer to this as "groupthink." In meetings, instead of taking action right away, I have observed that members would rather decide to wait a bit longer, see what happens, and then have another meeting. Even when in real trouble, many Japanese firms do not manage to take on radical decisions and turnarounds as easily as a Western firm. Japanese decision-making speed does not seem to be an issue because group processes dominate in a pressing issue. A friend who worked in Japan for many years once told me that Japanese managers "have all the time in the world." He referred to the fact that getting into business with Japanese companies can take a long time, sometimes years. And, yes, Japanese decision-making processes and, particularly, the time they take are creating major problems for Japanese management. Even today, when Japanese companies are getting more internationalized and know that they need to become faster in this area, it takes at least 3 times as long to come to a conclusion than in a Western firm.

Process Orientation

The Japanese love for process is evident in every Japanese firm. The love for details and patience makes Japanese employees a very reliable and dedicated workforce.

On the other hand, detailed processes need a lot of preparation and exercise, and have to be explained in great detail, to ensure they are performed well. If this is not the case, Japanese employees feel irritated and will constantly ask their peers or other team members for assistance. In many cases, questions are not asked directly, and it may take a while until misunderstandings become obvious.

Another negative aspect is the rigidness with which tasks are performed. Japanese employees perform their tasks flawlessly, but they will not change or improve them individually. It is hardly possible to change an operation or process (as bureaucratic, useless, or outdated as it might be) without involving other team members in this decision. This can lead to inflexibility and cross-cultural conflict. Western managers expect Japanese to work independently and to improve things individually if there is a need for it. Japanese employees, however, will not do so, as they will first consult other team members to make certain a little change will not influence others negatively.

Indirectness

The main difference between Western groups and Asian groups is the degree of trust within them. In Asia groups do not form easily and members are carefully chosen. In Asia, group members are responsible for each other, even if this means that not every individual wish can be fulfilled. Inside Japanese groups, harmonious relationships are a major goal. Conflicts or aggressive discussion need to be avoided at all costs. The reason for this is the long-term perspective of the group or organization. If people are not able to leave easily and are supposed to cooperate over the next 20 to 30 years, they need to get along in a nonaggressive way. So all members of a Japanese group prefer a climate of harmony and try to avoid open conflict. This is achieved by a very strong process orientation and a certain degree of indirectness. The following example is a very typical situation faced by Western managers working in a Japanese business environment.

A Japanese Team Meeting

Thomas is the head of the after-sales service department for a big European retailer in Japan. He has been in Japan for 2 years now and enjoys working there. He does not yet speak Japanese very well, so all other staff members have to speak to him in English. The company invests a lot of effort in developing its after-sales service and is, so far, quite content with Thomas's developments. However, it is clear that the company must work much harder to keep up with its Japanese competitors.

Thomas has decided to design new business processes to improve sales and after-sales services. He develops some initial ideas on how to improve the company's services and arranges a meeting to communicate his ideas to his Japanese colleagues. He is very excited about the meeting and presents his new ideas very enthusiastically. After this, he asks his team for feedback on his presentation. However, reactions are rather lukewarm. Most of his team members agree with his ideas, but he is left with the feeling that they do not really mean what they say. He then encourages his colleagues to criticize his ideas in the hope of creating a lively dis-cussion. This attempt also fails. His colleagues make some polite comments but do not really come up with radical new ideas.

After the meeting, Thomas feels very disappointed. He sees himself as a tolerant and open-minded boss and wants his team to discuss all aspects of work openly and freely. His Japanese team, however, seems to prefer to simply give polite comments and appears reluctant to openly discuss the pros and cons of new ideas.

Westerners working in Japan often will not encounter open resistance to a new idea or proposal. This does not mean that the idea is accepted, but many Japanese find it very difficult to openly confront others with their opinions. Even if encouraged to speak out, many Japanese will pre-fer to keep their thoughts to themselves. Here, the traditional commu-nication technique of *nemawashi* should be used. All members should be informed about a new idea beforehand either in a personal conver-sation or in a short memo. When directly talking to people about it, they can express their opinions about the topic and give feedback right away. Another possibility is to have team members write down their ideas before a meeting and then collect all the ideas before the discussion. All ideas can then be discussed more anonymously, and the feedback of the group will be more open.

Private and Professional Time Conflicts

In Japan, the distinction between private time and professional time is not always very clear. As mentioned earlier, many Japanese companies prefer their employees to attend company dinners and sports events and even send their staff on holiday together. Bonding and having friendlike, trust-intensive relationships between employees are seen as a means for improving the quality of work and for increasing motivation and over-all profits. Japanese employees are also expected to spend parts of their private time with their colleagues. From a Western perspective, however, this is not always desirable. Most Western managers prefer to spend their evenings with family and friends rather than at a company dinner.

Japanese employees in Western firms usually know this. They do not expect Western colleagues to join them if they plan a *nomikai* or weekend retreat. The problem that might occur in Japan, however, is that people who are not in attendance are considered antisocial and are suspected of not liking their colleagues. They also miss out on a lot of informal information about the firm. If the boss refuses to join these events, he or she might not be able to gain the trust of the team. The following case example describes a typical situation of a Western manager in Japan.

Socializing in Japan

Angelica was transferred from her head office in Europe to become the chief financial officer of her company's subsidiary in Japan. She was very excited about her new job and moved to Japan with a lot of enthusiasm. In her new office, she was the only foreigner and the only woman in a top management position.

During the first few weeks, she was busy finding her way around Japan and concentrated mostly on setting up her new household and getting used to her new life in Japan. Only after a few weeks was she able to concentrate more on her work and her colleagues.

Angelica observed that her colleagues spent time with each other after work. Angelica did not speak Japanese very well, so she often stayed away from these drinking and eating events. She also preferred to spend time with people from outside work because she found this more relaxing. She asked her colleagues out for lunch, but most of them preferred to eat from their lunch boxes in one of the meeting rooms or in a nearby park.

After 6 months in Japan, Angelica felt alienated from her colleagues. She tried to talk to them more, but they seemed reluctant to share information. It was difficult for her to obtain information, and they seemed to not trust her very much. She felt somewhat disconnected at the office and did not really know what to do.

In the 6 years that I spent in Japan, I heard similar stories many times. Westerners who do not appreciate socializing the "Japanese way" experience more negative consequences in business than they might expect. I usually suggest that they go out with their colleagues at least once a week. If they are invited out more, they should explain that a Western family does not appreciate this and apologize. But in my experience, joining colleagues once a week for a relaxed dinner is enough to create a friendly atmosphere and improve communication.

Kaizen Versus Radical Change

Japanese management is based on the premise of stability and slow, but steady, economic growth. It is not made for turbulent times in which drastic actions and decisions are needed. Managing and implementing radical changes is still a challenge for the Japanese firm where the *kaizen* principle still dominates thinking. As useful and efficient as the kaizen principle is for improving processes and quality, in times of crisis, corporations often require more radical changes. A radical change refers to a drastic action of improvement in a firm, such as a completely new strategy, job cuts, or rebranding.

Radical change, however, is difficult for Japanese firms. Since all decisions are made in the group and a large number of people are involved, decisions do not often lead to dramatically new ideas. Decisions made by the group should benefit many individuals (or many stakeholders). Radically new ideas often do not benefit many and are therefore not considered as suitable solutions in the Japanese firm. Western managers, on the other hand, are often sent to Japan to change and improve things in the local subsidiary. These different attitudes can lead to major communication problems and conflicts. The most successful approach is to show a lot of patience and change processes slowly but with persistence.

Dealing With Japanese Strategy Development

Another aspect that I find very problematic in Japanese firms is the inability of many Japanese managers to distinguish between strategic and operative decisions. Japanese business is very process oriented and places great importance on relationships within the firm and with the firm's stakeholders. Most Japanese managers are very busy on the operational level, carefully taking care of their relationships with colleagues and superiors. Strategic issues are often neglected in the Japanese firm, as Japanese managers prefer to deal with current issues and often miss a strategic vision.

This orientation is reflected in every company's activities and has its strengths and weaknesses. A good point is that it makes everybody stick to the rules and perform detailed processes very well. Japanese production management and service management greatly benefit from this attitude. In general, all production and service processes are fulfilled with great precision and care. Kaizen, just-in-time management, and other famous concepts are based on the Japanese love for details and well-performed processes.

The reasons for this can again be found in the structure of the Japanese group. No one can, or should, decide alone—many Japanese managers feel uncomfortable doing so and therefore a number of meetings must be called in order to make a decision. This is also the reason why processes, once established, will hardly be individually improved or changed, even if a process proves inefficient or even damaging to the firm. Without group consensus, nothing can be changed, and group consensus (with all its positive aspects) takes time. The relevance of the decision does not really matter. All decisions are group decisions in Japan. An American exchange student who held a part-time job as a waiter in a Japanese restaurant in Tokyo once told me that in the kitchen of the restaurant that he worked at, one of the chefs found that the dishwashing liquid was not located in the best possible place. Instead of just putting it somewhere else, as my student would have done, he called two of his colleagues, and they discussed the issue for about 10 minutes and then finally decided together where to put the liquid from now on. It should be in a place where everybody can easily reach it, my astonished student was told.

Senpai-Kôhai Relationships in a Western Firm

In the West, new recruits are expected to take responsibility from the very first day when entering the firm. They have to show their motivation and ability and have to find their role within their team, department, or organization. Being successful in a Western team mostly depends on the individual's ability to actively influence this process.

In Japan, the *senpai-kôhai* system leads to completely different behavior. Young recruits are expected to socialize by obeying and learning from their older colleagues. They mostly do this by watching them, taking on easy tasks at the beginning, and being taken care of by their *senpai*. Being successful in a Japanese team means being more passive and listening to older peers. In the context of a Japanese firm, being active in finding a role and taking on an independent task is considered very inappropriate in general and unheard of for beginners. This behavior often leads to intercultural conflict.

Foreign Women Working in Japanese Firms

Japanese companies are becoming more open to non-Japanese employees. The main reason is the increasing need to internationalize a foreign workforce that can support business activities within international markets. As the number of foreigners working in Japanese firms is increasing, the percentage of foreign women in firms is rising as well. International women are mostly hired for the same reasons as foreign men: They offer specialized skills increasingly needed in Japanese firms.

Integrating Women Into the Workforce

Japanese companies still hold a comparatively low number of female managers. Only around 10% of managerial positions are held by women in Japan, compared to 42% in the United States and 35% in the United Kingdom.[2] Until recently, Japanese women were not given equal opportunities in terms of either payment or the possibility of having successful careers in their home country.

Future Managers Versus Administrative Staff

Japanese companies divide their employees into two groups, with each performing very different tasks and entertaining different career prospects. One group is known as *sôgôshoku* (managerial track) and the other as *ippanshoku* (administrative track). Employees chosen for the *sôgôshoku* track are assigned comprehensive tasks and are expected to develop analytical and managerial skills. They are the only ones who can make a managerial career within the firm.

The *ippanshoku* track employees are assigned clerical tasks and support employees in the managerial track. Their tasks will include everything from photocopying to greeting customers to serving tea at meetings. They remain "peripheral and subordinate workers with lower wages, [and] management does not expect them to performing [*sic*] demanding functions or follow a career path."[3] These kinds of job exist in Western companies, too, and many administrative tasks are performed by women. In Japan, however, the situation is a bit different. University graduates are chosen for both tracks, and the company decides which tracks prospective employees enter and will stay in. Once an employee is on the administrative track, she will stay there and has almost no chance of being promoted into a more suitable position.

In Japan, the *ippanshoku* track is mainly reserved for women, whereas the *sôgôshoku* track is mostly for men. Even in 2008, only 6% of *sôgôshoku* employees were women—an extremely low number. The number of newly hired women for the *sôgôshoku* track in the same year was a bit higher (16.9%). These numbers show that even today, many female university graduates are not given equal employment opportunities in Japan. Females still dominate the *ippanshoku* track, with 93% of women employed in such positions in 2008.[4]

Next to these company traditions, there are a number of other issues that make having a career difficult for Japanese women. There is still a wage gap between male and female employees, and working hours are long, making it very difficult for women with families to maintain a career. The Japanese tax system also hinders women's careers because it provides tax exemptions for married women who are earning less than 1,300,000 yen (US$14,200) per year.[5]

Negative Consequences

The gender division within the Japanese labor market has very negative consequences for business and for the Japanese economy. First of all, about half of educated Japanese are not fully integrated into the labor market, and the number of women in part-time positions is extraordinarily high. Another effect is—quite unexpectedly—the low birth rate. Despite the strict distinction between motherhood and work life, the Japanese birth rate is one of the lowest in the world. Studies have shown that in countries where female participation in the labor market is high and is supported by the government, the fertility rate is high as well.

There have been some half-hearted attempts by the Japanese government to improve the situation. An equal employment law was enacted in 1986 to support equal career opportunities for women, but the law has shown little effect so far. It allows Japanese companies to make individual interpretations of the law and does not guarantee equal opportunities for men and women within the firm. The responsibility to improve this situation therefore lies with Japanese firms. They have increasingly realized that gender issues are a managerial problem and have started to change many of their traditional practices, providing day-care facilities and flex time and even abolishing the *ippanshoku* track. Integrating women into the Japanese workforce, and giving them equal opportunities to have successful careers and a happy family life, will be the utmost challenge for the Japanese firm in the 21st century.

Gender Issues

In general, Western women working in Japanese firms are considered "honorary males" and are seen as very emancipated and direct in performance and speech. I have always had the impression that the Japanese think women have a much stronger position in firms in Western countries than is actually the case, an attitude that helps women working in Japan. This privilege, however, does not apply to women of other ethnicities when working in Japan, who may face strong prejudice in a Japanese work environment. Neither does it imply that Japanese women are treated in the same way; often, they still have to face discrimination, while Western women are able to perform managerial tasks. Having a successful long-term career in a Japan may be problematic, however. The number of cases in which non-Japanese employees entered top management in Japan is still low for both sexes. In general, promotions may take a long time and are not based on achievement, as they are in the West.

Marketing Strategy

Being a Western woman in Japan has a very positive marketing effect. Since there are only a few of us, most Japanese business partners do remember our names and affiliation. A friend who worked in the wood industry also said that being the only Western woman in Japan in this industry helped her to create a lot of business. Most potential business partners were very interested in meeting and getting to know her, out of curiosity, at first, but a lot of these meetings developed into good business relationships. Even years later, she comments, people would remember her name.

Networking Groups

As the number of foreign women in Japan is increasing, the possibility of meeting and networking with professional international women in Japan has also increased. The following networking groups target international women in Japan (mostly in the Tokyo area):

- *FEW (Foreign Executive Women)* is a networking group for Japanese and Western women. The group also has a Kansai chapter and meets once a month. Their website is http://www .fewjapan.com.
- *AWF (Association of Women in Finance)* is a networking group for men and women interested in finance and international business in Japan. Meetings always feature a prominent guest speaker. Their website is http://www.awftokyo.com.
- *FWLA (Foreign Women Lawyers' Association)* is a networking group focusing on the legal professions. Meetings feature a guest speaker on a variety of topics. Their website is http:// www2.gol.com/users/fwla/.
- *Being A Broad in Japan* is a networking group founded by British author and publisher Caroline Pover. Meetings focus on networking and usually do not involve a speech. The group also has its own magazine called *Being A Broad in Japan*, which provides information and support for international women in Japan. Their website is http://www.being-a-broad.com.

Summary

- Working in Japan as a non-Japanese manager is accompanied by numerous intercultural and often very challenging experiences. At the beginning of an international career in Japan, language problems cause the main frustration. Japanese is not a language to be learned within a year or two; in most cases, employees do not show a high level of English skills.

- Challenges to managing in Japan are mostly intercultural. Indirect and nonconfrontational communication styles are often misunderstood by Western managers. Communication patterns also differ in Japan. Japanese employees often communicate in an indirect and nonverbal way. Conflicts and misunderstandings are therefore difficult to solve.

- Marked emphasis on the group over the individual in Japan is another aspect of Japanese culture that presents challenges to international managers. This leads to long-lasting discussions and little individual responsibility. Japanese employees are also highly process oriented, which is positive if the company is involved in manufacturing or service management but can be a problem once business processes need to be changed or improved quickly.

- Another cultural issue is the Japanese tendency to mix private and professional life. Japanese workers generally do not make a clear distinction between private and professional time, and they tend to spend more time with their colleagues after work. Many Japanese companies encourage their employees to meet after work and on weekends. This is meant to improve teamwork and the relationships between coworkers; however, this often conflicts with non-Japanese managers' ideas about separating private and professional life.

- Another issue in Japanese management is the emphasis on process orientation and the fact that every decision, even the smallest one, can only be made if all others are included. Misunderstandings also occur when Western and Japanese ideas about how to change processes and strategies collide.

- International women face fewer challenges when working in a Japanese firm than expected. In many cases, Western women are seen as "honorary males" or more as "foreigners" than specifically as women. Being the only Western women in a firm can also come with marketing advantages. International women in Japanese management are still rare, so they are usually remembered.

CHAPTER 8

Selling Your Product to Japanese Customers

In contrast to Japanese production management and human resource management, Japanese marketing has never been a topic discussed by Western media or researchers. The reasons for this are not quite clear, but I assume that cultural differences or language barriers seemed too great. Especially in Tokyo, marketing is constantly evolving, often innovative, and always competitive. In Tokyo alone, there are more than a million enterprises and 160,000 restaurants competing for the attention of around 35 million consumers. Trends come and go on a weekly basis.[1]

The main pillars of Japanese marketing are excellent customer service, high product quality and innovation, and a strong sensibility toward consumer trends and the needs of new customer groups. Japanese consumers are considered the most sophisticated in the world and are accustomed to zero product defects and perfect and free-of-charge service. For foreign investors, marketing and adapting to Japanese consumers is therefore often the greatest challenge when entering the market. This chapter will provide you with an overview of the basic aspects of marketing in Japan and provide some tips on how to improve market recognition of your goods. Upon completion of this chapter you should be able understand the following points:

- How Japanese marketing differs from the West
- What the particularities of Japanese consumer behavior are
- What consumer groups are most prominent in the Japanese market
- How Japanese companies market their products
- What "dos and don'ts" exist in marketing in Japan

The Best Service in the World

In Japan, customers are called *O-kyaku-sama*. The word *kyaku* means guest or customer, and the prefix *O* and the suffix *sama* are honorific expressions for showing politeness and respect to a potential client. The relationship between buyer and seller is therefore a hierarchical one in which the customer always holds all power.[2] Customer needs always come first in a Japanese firm; professional friendliness is expected of all employees. After entering the firm, each new hire receives extensive training on how to communicate with customers. Rules are often very detailed, explaining exactly how to bow and how to exchange name cards, for example.

Japanese consumers expect the best service procedures in the world. The concept of service in Japan greatly differs from that in the West. In Japan, good service means that customers' wishes are taken care of in any possible way. When entering a Japanese shop, one will be greeted by at least one or two shop clerks, who are first investigating whether the customer would like to get some information on the product or whether he really wants to purchase it. Waiting times, unless there are really big crowds, can hardly be found. Every interaction with customers is of great importance, because Japanese consumers react to "bad service" very quickly. Brand loyalty is very low, and once a shop or product does not fulfill basic requirements, it is easily exchanged for another one. For Western corporations entering the Japanese market, this means that all service activities must be adapted to Japanese expectations.

Shinhatsubai (New on Sale)

Japanese customers also have a strong influence on the firm's product and service development decisions. Japanese corporations constantly have to develop new products to keep the interest of Japanese consumers.

Asian consumers generally show a higher diffusion rate than Western consumers, which means that they are more interested and more likely to buy new products or products that reflect new technology. Japanese consumers are no exception. Diffusion of innovations—the process whereby a new product, service, or idea spreads among a population[3]—is very high in Japan. Once a brand has gained acceptance among early adopters, the rate of diffusion proceeds rapidly in societies with homogenous cultural and socioeconomic backgrounds like Japan.[4] Not surprisingly, Japanese consumers are also very technology oriented and prefer to buy products that are technologically state of the art.[5] Today, adapting products to consumer wishes is one of a Japan's lasting strengths. New product development is characterized by a strong focus on satisfying consumers' wishes. This is partly explained by group orientation but also can be called a Japanese management strategy. This strategy became evident during the rapid development of the Japanese economy after Japan opened up in 1853. The Japanese have always been very interested in outside ideas, and they have a great talent for integrating foreign ideas into their culture and businesses. Today, this interest in new and exciting products means Japanese consumers are also willing to pay a lot of money for them. Companies in Japan react by constantly launching new products. New products are labeled *shinhatsubai*, which means "new on sale" or "new release," and Japanese consumers preferably buy these newly released products.[6] Not all of these products are real and radical innovations—nor do they provide a completely new value to customers. In many cases, these "new" products are often simply new flavors or packages.

Gentei (Limited Edition)

Another particular feature of Japanese manufacturing is *gentei* (special editions), which are product adaptations that are only sold for a limited period of time. Many *gentei* are only on sale for a month, and most usually reflect the time of the year. Most *gentei* can be found in food products, and every year, we are surprised by various entertaining flavors of famous brands. Even brands that are not Japanese adopted this trend. Most famous for its *gentei* is the Kit Kat, the famous chocolate bar. It has been available in every flavor imaginable, such as apple, passion fruit, pumpkin, and mango pudding. The more exotic versions of the chocolate bar include green tea, apple vinegar, and vegetable. Other Western brands followed. Coca-Cola presents a cool summer edition every year (e.g., blue Hawaii or *Shizo*, an herb used to flavor raw fish).

As crazy as these new flavors sound to the conservative palate, the *gentei* are very successful instruments in strengthening and rejuvenating a brand product. In most cases, the new editions are not even supported by any advertising campaign, but they create interest anyway. Loyal customers have another reason to buy their favorite brands and not-yet customers are also inclined to try the new flavor. Limited editions maintain interest in the brand, refresh its image, and keep the public talking and blogging and interested in them.

The Relevance of Brands

Brands play an important role in the Japanese consumer market. Japanese consumers have a high affinity for expensive brands, and the Japanese market is often called the only luxury mass market in the world. This attitude was challenged a bit during the economic crisis of 2008, but nevertheless, expensive brand products are important for showing status and success in Japanese society. The term *burando* (brand) refers only to luxury products such as bags and fashion and not to products of more casual brands such as skin care or other products.

Some Western brands even manage to reposition their image in the Japanese market. Wella, a German hair care corporation with a mass-market position in Europe, has emerged as the most expensive shampoo brand in the Japanese market, completely adapting their products to Japanese taste.

Another particularity of Japanese marketing is the fact that company brands dominate over product brands. Japanese consumers traditionally tend to choose mostly large, well-known companies such as Mitsubishi or Yamaha, for example. Thus, consumers believe they can avoid making the wrong decision or buying an inferior product since purchasing a new brand from an unknown company might result in dissatisfaction.[7] Schuette and Ciarlante propose that "image-building in Japan is not limited to a brand but is in most cases linked with the corporate image."[8] That is why Japanese advertising often focuses more on the company than on the product.[9] The company and its reputation play a major role in influencing the buying decision. At the end of television spots, the company producing the product is mentioned. In the following sidebar, we can see an overview of the particularities when marketing in Japan.

Particularities of Marketing in Japan

- Service is always the best in the world and for free.
- The focus is on innovative and technology-oriented products.
- There is a constant development of new products or limited editions (even in less innovation-oriented industries).
- Company brands dominate over product brands.
- Mobile marketing is a major marketing instrument.

The Japanese Consumer

The most important player in Japanese marketing is the consumer. Japan is a country with "more than 120 million affluent customers,"[10] and of all the countries in Asia, Japan is the most seasoned in consumerism.[11] Until a few years ago, Japanese consumers were seen as a homogenous group with one language, a flat income distribution, and relatively high educational levels.[12] As far as class or income and race are concerned, there does not seem to be much heterogeneity since most of the Japanese belong to the middle class and the consumer market consists predominantly of Japanese.[13] Over the past several years, changes in the Japanese economy have led to increasing changes in Japanese society and to the emergence of new and profitable customer groups.

Japan's Emerging Consumer Groups

Japan and its companies work on responding quickly to satisfy the demands of each demographic group and to offer tailor-made products. Japanese new product development includes the desires of customers and shows great openness to very small ideas. This section provides an overview of the most widely discussed new consumer groups in Japan.

The New Rich

Even if Japan claims to be a middle-class society and most Japanese perceive themselves as middle class, Japan is developing into a class society. At the same time as the number of part-time workers in Japan is dramatically rising and their income is going down, there is an increasing number of people in Japan who are very wealthy. Japanese media call this group the new rich, or *fuyuso*.

The Baby Boomers

Japan has, by far, the oldest population in Asia and the world's most rapidly aging society. Currently, Japan has the oldest population in the world.[14] As problematic as this development is for the future of the Japanese society and economy, Japanese companies have long recognized the silver generation as a profitable target group. The most discussed group is the baby boomer; in Japan, this group is also called the *dankei* generation. The baby boomers are Japanese born between 1947 and 1949, before the birth rate started to decline from 1950 on.[15] Members of this group are known as the "typical Japanese": married, successful—but not too successful—middle-class white-collar workers. They accumulated large sums through saving, so they have much money to spend and, upon retiring, time to spend it. This group mainly spends money on travel, health, and fashion. After a lifetime in the same corporation, many of them are entitled to retirement money of up to 36 months of their former salary.

Working Women and the Single Market

Since the 1970s, more and more Japanese women have entered the workforce. This does not mean that they all pursue successful careers, but since the wage level in Japan is comparatively high, they have also become a profitable target group. Many Japanese women may put off marriage until their late 20s or even 30s in order to enjoy their single years with high disposable incomes.[16] An increasing number of Japanese women do not get married at all, a phenomenon that was only recently discovered by Japanese marketers. Japanese women turned into the world's most visible and highly regarded consumers,[17] and working women in Japan have a major impact on Japanese consumption. Nonmarried women especially tend to live with their parents, which decreases the cost of housing and leaves them with more money to spend. They have been termed "parasite singles" since they are famous for spending a high part of their income on fashion and overseas travel. Another group of single women—those over 30 who are willingly or unwillingly not married—also entered the focus of attention in the past years. The public calls them *makeinu* (loser dogs) based on the novel *Makeinu no toboe* (The Howl of the Loser Dog) by Junko Sakai in which she describes her lonely, single life in Tokyo. Despite this shameful name, single women have received a lot of attention by the media and marketers over the past years, and many Japanese firms have started to directly address them with customized products.

Otaku

Otaku is Japanese term that is also often used outside of Japan to refer to people with obsessive interests—particularly Japanese animation, *manga*, and video games—generally believed to be very knowledgeable in their area of interest. The word *otaku* can best be equated to the English words "nerd," "geek," or "fanboy." Even if its usage in Japanese society is also understood to mean someone who has an antisocial personality, serious devotees of Japanese subculture are often called *otaku*.

The word "otaku" in standard Japanese is a very formal way of saying "you," roughly equivalent to the English "thou." It was adopted by hardcore Japanese fans of *manga* and animé (comics and animation, respectively) in the early 1980s as a slang term referring to them. The terms have broadened in recent years to refer to fanatics of any number of hobbies, from car enthusiasts to collectors of *manga*-inspired dolls. What makes the *otaku* market so peculiar is that consumption behavior is driven by sympathy, admiration, and pursuit of "ideals" (i.e., creating fan fiction based on their interpretations) as well as the orientation toward forming a strong community that is hardly approachable by ordinary people.[18]

There is one common characteristic of all the different *otaku* groups—they spend most of their free time, and a lot of money, on their preferred hobby. The stereotypical otaku is an unmarried male professional, usually working in a technology-related field, though this stereotype is hardly universal. *Otaku* range from young to old, male and female, and indulge in various hobbies. Typical *otaku* hobbies are comics and animation, video games, and electronics of all types. Five major classifications make up the bulk of the *otaku* market: comics (100 billion yen annually), animation (20 billion yen), idols (60 billion yen), games (78 billion yen), and PC assembly (32 billion yen). The *otaku* market covers various market segments and consists of many small niche markets that serve the particular tastes of the fanatics of that specific interest. Nomura Research Institute[19] claims that over 2.85 million Japanese could be categorized as otaku and that this market segment generates over $2.6 billion annually. Comic books (the largest of these *otaku* markets, at over 350,000 people) are generating revenues to the tune of 83 billion yen per year.

Japanese Consumer Behavior

Group Oriented or Not?

In collectivist-oriented cultures, product and brand preferences are more likely to express attitudes arising from social norms than from internal drives or motives. Thus, "loyalty is a key concept in collectivist cultures" and the "unusual level of single brand dominance in many Asian markets" is due to the fact that Asian consumers tend to "rely more on information found in their reference group" and tend to "follow the group consensus until there is significant evidence showing that the new product is better."[20] Besides, most Asian cultures show a propensity toward uncertainty or risk avoidance, which often results in consumer behavior exhibiting high brand-name consciousness, a greater insistence on quality, the active use of reference groups and opinion leaders, group shopping, and a slower acceptance of new products.[21] Over the past several years, there has been a tendency to differentiate by buying more individualized products. These products, however, still have to exhibit high quality and should preferably be a brand product.

Quality Obsession

The Japanese are obsessed with "quality," and "to the Japanese within everything there is an inherent state of perfection and harmony."[22] The Japanese generally assume that the quality of Japanese products is higher than that of Western products, and they are willing to pay higher prices for them, too. One reason for this is a high level of after-sale services, which are a common thing for Japanese companies but are often not expected or received by foreign producers. In Japan, quality therefore permeates every aspect of a product and involves continuous attention to improvement.[23]

Low Brand Loyalty

We have already witnessed on several occasions that the Japanese differ from other Asian consumers in their consumer behavior. In fact, it is generally believed that Japanese consumers do not tend to be brand loyal. Schuette and Ciarlante[24] point out that Japanese consumers "did not actively seek out or try new brands" and that this type of consumer is still prevalent in Japan, particularly in the older segment of the population.[25] And yes, traditional Japanese consumers tend to stay loyal to a company they are buying from but not necessarily to the brand itself.[26] However, this does not mean that brand name does not play any role in the purchase decision. On the contrary, the brand might very often be important. However, the Japanese do not necessarily stay with the same brand for a long time, attaching priority to—once again—service, product quality, and technology.[27]

Technology Orientation

Japanese consumers are also very technology oriented and electronic-gadget oriented.[28] Not only are service and product quality expected to be high end, but technology has to be cutting edge as well. However, Japanese people do not like to have their lifestyles changed by technology; instead, they skillfully apply technology to their traditional lifestyle. Japanese people are very curious and interested in innovations and new developments in technology. They have an affinity for buying new products, especially when they offer some new functions or features.

Price Sensitivity

Traditionally, Japanese consumers show little price sensitivity. If service, quality, and technology meet the expectations of the Japanese consumer, he or she is willing to pay a high price as well. Prices may be perceived as indicators of quality. Schuette and Ciarlante[29] argue that "the reliance on price as an indicator of quality is most critical in the case of purchases of products that affect the standing of the individual within the peer group," and, "thus, the price-quality equation serves as a risk-reduction mechanism for the uninformed." Since a customer's association of higher prices with higher quality is apparently quite strong in Japan, this might be one explanation for the lack of price sensitivity.

The economic crisis of 2008 has also changed this attitude a little. It is increasingly popular to purchase "cheaper" (nonluxury) brands, especially among young Japanese consumers.

Reacting to Consumer Evolution: New Trends in Japanese Marketing

Consumers and Product Design

Consumers are increasingly interested in customized and individualized products. Business models that help customers design their own products are booming. As consumers are seeking out more unique and personalized products, they are also interested in customizing the products they buy. Some brands even go a step further and include customers in their product-design processes. Soup manufacturer Maruchan and beverage company Calpis even let their consumers vote on their favorite flavors each year.

Integrating customers in product development processes comes with rewards. Customers feel more attached to the products and show more interest in the overall brand. Meanwhile, the company can create greater customer feedback and launch campaigns that specifically target their customers' wishes and ideas.

Simplifying Product Choices

Tokyo is the biggest market place in the world, overflowing with new offers and products. But in other places around the world, the number and speed of new products being introduced is dramatically increasing. More and more consumers find it difficult to make purchase decisions simply because they are worried about buying the wrong product or about missing a bargain they have not yet discovered. These overwhelmed consumers tend to buy products later or to not buy them at all. This is a trend not only in Tokyo but also in most industrialized countries.

Shoppers are feeling increasingly out of the loop when it comes to new products and the advanced technologies that often accompany them.

The Japanese have realized this buyer dilemma and have started developing products or business models that support customers in making quick and simple purchase decisions. KDDI, one of Japan's leading mobile communications provider, for example, introduced the Kantan Keitai, a mobile phone that strips away all the complicated and high-tech gadgets that are standard for most Japanese mobile phones these days. The company's target group is consumers who simply want to buy and use the talk feature of a mobile phone.

Simple and low-risk product choices are the base of Ranking-Ranqueen's business model. The company targets consumers who might shy away from buying simply because the choice of potential products is too massive. Based on the best seller of its parent company, the Tokyu department store chain, Ranking-Ranqueen produces a ranking of the most popular products each week. The hit products in each category are announced in the shops and consumers do not have to think about which product is the best. The concept has already been copied by big retail chains, which also started to point out their best-selling products. This technique lowers customers' risks of buying a product that might turn out to be wrong or of low quality. Customers show higher satisfaction with their purchases and place greater trust in the company.

Social Networks Go Offline

As in every major city, Tokyo has a growing number of customers who live alone. The number of single households or households without children in Tokyo has steadily increased over the past several years. People are increasingly lonely and desire more social interaction and contact with one another.

This request is being answered by Japanese companies that are creating social networking beyond the "classic" Internet networks. They are trying to connect consumers in real life. Leading in this field are the numerous Japanese railway companies. The Seibu Train Company started their first "hiking day" a few years ago, and Tokyo Metro and other major railway lines around the capital soon followed this practice. The companies organize guided tours in certain locations for all interested customers. These events are free but have developed a seri-ously growing fan base.

Another famous example of a social network developed by a company is the sports-goods producer Asics. The company is famous for sponsor-ing the Tokyo sightseeing run, which covers all major sights of Tokyo in a 15-km run. Other runs target women, beginners, and early morning runners, and runs are offered every day. Again, all of these events are free of charge, but it is evident that consumers become avid fans of them and, eventually, of the companies offering them.

Social meetings between consumers also support difficult purchase decisions. For instance, Tokyo real estate developers offer seminars for women (their new target group) who plan to buy apartments. These sem-inars allow potential buyers to meet each other and often lead to more positive purchase decisions in the end. Connecting consumers has a posi-tive effect on a company's long-term strategy. Consumers become fans of the brand, which, in turn, will positively influence their purchasing decisions in the future.

"Dos" When Marketing a Product in Japan

Marketing a Western product in Japan is often considered a challenging task. In fact, Western investors who bring quality products to the Japa-nese market enjoy a lot of benefits and strategic advantages. The follow-ing section will provide some insights on how non-Japanese marketers can succeed in Japan.

Bring the Right Product

Japan is often seen as a market in which any Western product can be sold. Today, however, Japan is, by far, one of the most competitive markets in the world. Japanese consumers are the most sophisticated, and they are accustomed to the highest quality and high service levels. In contrast to other Asian markets, such as China, there is mostly a very strong and well-established Japanese competitor for each product in Japan. Foreign-ness alone does not guarantee success.

However, market entries can be very successful if the product or ser-vice to be brought to Japan is unique or presents an added value to the consumer that Japanese products do not. This means that the product to be presented to the Japanese audience needs to be chosen well. Brand products or patents can still create a lot of interest among Japanese consumers. More challenging than entering the market successfully is keeping the interest of Japanese consumers. As we now understand, Japanese consumers are used to new products and innovation all the time. Competition is tough and establishing a brand for the long term in Japan is a more challenging managerial task than entering the market with an interesting products and celebrating instant sales success.

Use the Gaijin Bonus

Foreign firms face many challenges in the Japanese market. The highest hurdle is fulfilling the expectations of Japanese customers. Foreignness can also be an advantage. A Western company creates a lot of interest in the Japanese market, especially if the product is a brand product or shows a particular added value. Marketing and public relations (PR) are often easier than expected.

In an interview series I did a few years ago with CEOs of corporations in Japan, all interviewees confirmed that being a foreigner could be very positive for the business. Non-Japanese managers do not always have to play by Japanese rules; they can, for example, be more direct when initiating the first business contact. The Japanese are very interested in foreign products and new ideas in general. This is also the case for the Japanese media, which react a lot more positively to PR activities surrounding new products than many Western media firms (given that an interesting product is being introduced).

Professional Networking and Lobbying

Japan is a society in which communities and groups play a very important role. Diffusion and acceptance of new products is very high; once an early majority of customers is reached, the market can be quickly penetrated.

A lot of business in Japan is done via introductions by business partners or personal relationships. Being introduced to other business people and developing friendly relationships with potential business partners is a major part of Japanese business practice. The Japanese are very professional networkers, and Tokyo particularly offers a great variety of business-related networking events. For Western investors, these events provide a great opportunity to meet potential business partners.

Networking events are usually organized by the local chambers of commerce or local networking groups and have a certain time limit (usually 2 hours) so all attendees can still catch the last train. Their fees vary between 3000 (US$30) to 5000 yen (US$50). Typically, food is served and participants actively talk to each other and exchange name cards.

Table 8.1 provides an overview of the most popular networking groups for foreign investors and managers in Japan.

"Don'ts" When Marketing a Product in Japan

Despite the advantages that foreignness can bring, when marketing a product in Japan, there are some mistakes that have to be avoided at all costs. The main problem of foreign products in Japan is their quality level, which is usually much lower than their Japanese counterparts. The following sections describe mistakes that are frequently made by foreign investors.

Keeping the Home Country's Service Level

Japanese customers are accustomed to the best service in the world. All service activities in Japan are based on the idea of convenience (*benrisa*) and safety (*anzen*). Especially in the big cities, consumers are used to cooperative and supportive staff in shops, zero delays in delivery, and free after-sales service based on professional friendliness.

These are basic requirements, and Japanese consumers also expect them from foreign firms in Japan. For a Western corporation, these expectations are often rather challenging because their procedures, even if considered good or superior to customers in the West, need to adapt to Japanese standards in any case.

Ignoring Quality Defects

The high expectation of good services is accompanied by the lowest tolerance of quality problems. Japanese consumers, and also Japanese business

Table 8.1. Networking Organizations for Foreign Entrepreneurs and Managers in Tokyo

Entrepreneur Association of Tokyo	http://www.ea-tokyo.com	Organization that promotes and encourages greater entrepreneurship in Japan. Holds monthly meetings and seminars with regular guest speakers
Foreign Correspondents' Club of Japan (FCCJ)	http://www.fccj.or.jp	Club that offers networking opportunities and organizes speeches with very international guest speakers
Pink Cow Connections	http://www.thepink cow.com/	Organization that encourages business networking and professional development. Based out of the Pink Cow restaurant in Tokyo
Black Professionals in Tokyo	http://blackprofessionals tokyo.ning.com	Networking organization for Black professionals in Tokyo; also assists members with business development
German Institute for Japanese Studies	http://www.dijtokyo.org/	Research organization that examines business and cultural issues in Japan and also aims to promote a greater relationship between Japan and Germany. Holds seminars and workshops on a regular basis
Endeavor Japan	http://www.endeavour -japan.org	Organization that holds seminars and workshops on various issues in Japan
Japan Venture Capital Association	http://www.jvca.jp	Organization that promotes greater venture capital in Japan
Waseda Marketing Forum	http://www.waseda marketing.com	Organization at Waseda University in Tokyo that promotes networking and business discussions in Japan
Temple University Institute of Contemporary Asian Studies	http://www.tuj.ac.jp	Organization at Temple University Japan Campus in Tokyo that holds seminars, conferences, and workshops on various issues in Asia
Sophia University Institute of Comparative Culture	http://www.fla.sophia .ac.jp/icc/index.htm	Organization at Sophia University in Tokyo that holds seminars and lectures on various topics in Japan

customers, are obsessed with quality; therefore, quality is the key to success in the Japanese market. Most Japanese manufacturers focus very strongly on producing the best possible products. The high expectations of Japanese consumers were a major factor in developing Japanese production management styles (see chapter 3).

A Western organization, on the other hand, can afford a defect rate of 2% or even a bit higher. If consumers purchase a product below their expectations, they will return it and receive a new product and sometimes a coupon or gift on top of this. As long as product defects do not occur too often, consumers will accept this procedure and will not leave for a new supplier. In the Japanese context, this is not acceptable. Japanese corporations will always aim at zero-percent product defects because their consumers will not accept any defects.

One CEO described that after delivering a defective product to a business customer, the company replaced it immediately and apologized. Even if the process were unusually fast by Western standards, their customers would remember the incident even 3 years later and would mention it at every business meeting.

Summary

- Japanese marketing exhibits some particular features, such as a great love for service and a strong customer orientation. Japanese consumers show a high affinity for new products and technologies and show little brand loyalty. Two popular ways to increase and sustain consumer interest in Japan are product adaptations (*shinhatsubai*) and special editions (*gentei*).
- The Japanese market mainly consists of middle-class consumers, but several new consumer groups are gathering the attention of media and marketers. The new rich are Japan's affluent consumers, who have started to show their wealth by purchasing expensive designer goods. Japan's large silver market has stimulated its economy and made it a leader in product development for older consumers. Two groups neglected for many years are working women and young and middle-aged consumers who live in a single household. The *otaku* (enthusiastic

consumers) market is another target group that increasingly creates interest among Japanese marketers.

- When marketing products as a foreigner in Japan, it is advisable to bring the right product and to use the advantages foreigners have in the Japanese market. They are more easily recognized and remembered and can use many networking opportunities only created for them. Mistakes to be avoided are keeping the home country's quality level and allowing even minimal product defects.

- New trends in Japanese marketing increasingly involve consumers in new product development, simplifying product choices for overwhelmed consumers and supporting consumer groups in going offline and communicating in daily life.

CHAPTER 9

Negotiations With Japanese Business Partners

When negotiating with Japanese business partners, cultural differences become most obvious. Japanese negotiation techniques include building strong relationships with their business partners, vague responses, and group decision making. Western negotiation styles are therefore often perceived as aggressive and too direct. Many negotiations fail because of these cross-cultural misunderstandings. Knowledge of basic Japanese negotiation practices can help in reaching goals and supporting market-entry processes. The following sections discuss the mistakes to avoid when negotiating with Japanese business partners. Upon completion of this chapter you will learn about the following factors:

- Why personal relationships between business partners play such an important role in Japan
- How to start a business negotiation in Japan
- How to contact a potential client in Japan
- How Japanese meetings are held and which aspects are most important
- How to recognize the most powerful negotiator in a Japanese meeting
- Why Japanese business dinners and karaoke parties are so important for business

Avoiding Conflict

Confucianism is more of a social code for behavior than it is a religion. It is goes back to the philosopher Confucius, who believed that stability

and peace could only be achieved by the correct management of interpersonal relationships. Harmony is a major goal to achieve, and loyalty
and compromise can support it. Shintoism, which stresses harmony
with the earth, is Japan's only indigenous religion. Loyalty and harmony with one's environment also play a major role in Shintoism. Bud-
dhism, which focuses on tolerance and spiritual equality, was imported
to Japan from China.[1]

These three philosophies are still observed in many East Asian countries today, and they make human relationships the primary concern of
the Japanese. Respect for elders, filial piety, and loyalty are promoted in
Japan. The Japanese are deeply influenced by loyalty to their peers, family, and organizations. Harmony must be kept at all costs.

Personal Relationships Are Most Important

Japanese firms generally prefer doing business with partners they
know—the longer the relationship, the better. Japanese business partners prefer personal contact with their clients and their suppliers and
will traditionally spend quite a lot of time developing relationships
with them. They are also famous for paying a higher price and staying
with a well-known supplier rather than switching to a cheaper one.
Many Western firms consider this overloyal attitude as a barrier to
market entry.

The recession and increasing competition have changed all of this.
Japanese companies are less reluctant to do business with new partners;
however, personal relationships still play an important role, and Japanese
managers will always feel more comfortable once a friendly relationship is
established. In Japan, developing good relationships with clients and suppliers is seen as part of the job. Usually, time will be reserved after work
for company dinners or karaoke parties.

First Contact With Japanese Business Partners

The business literature on Japanese negotiations generally advises one to
behave as Japanese as possible when attempting to contact a Japanese company for the first time. Japanese companies usually do not do "cold calls"
or e-mails but instead prefer introductions via third parties or companies.

Usually, it is recommended that Western firms get into contact with a firm via a third party or one of the local chambers of commerce in Tokyo. Fairs and networking events provide good opportunities for making contacts with local corporations; such events are frequently organized in Tokyo.

The current business environment has relaxed things a bit. In general, Japanese companies expect Western firms to operate differently from Japanese firms. Cold calls from Western firms are becoming more common in Japan; these should be performed in a polite manner. Selling too directly is never a good idea in Japan.

It is often advised that the first business communication should be in Japanese, especially if you are planning to cooperate with a traditional firm where employees may not be accustomed to or confident when communicating in English. A Japanese business letter makes a better first impression and eases contact right from the beginning. Business Japanese is a very delicate issue, and the levels of politeness must be considered very carefully. It is further advisable to hire a professional business translator to write and translate the letter.

Today in Japan, more business in done in English. Depending on the client (some prefer to speak Japanese), English letters, e-mails, and introductions may be an adequate way of addressing a new client. Generally, one can say that the more traditional the industry, the better it is to write a Japanese letter. In young industries or companies that do a lot of business overseas, the firm can also be introduced in English.

For foreign investors, the possibility of speaking English eases business, but in the long run, it is necessary to have native Japanese speakers taking over tasks that follow the first business contacts. Even if Japanese companies are interested in cooperating with a Western firm, they sometimes fear communication problems or cultural misunderstandings. Bringing a Japanese employee signalizes that future business can be done in the Japanese language and according to Japanese business customs. A Japanese colleague can further clarify misunderstandings right after the meeting and improve overall communications with a client.

Meeting Culture in Japan

Japanese meetings are called *kaigi*. *Kaigi* are still one of the most important management operations in Japan, but their intention and meaning completely differs from the Western meeting. In the West, meetings are held to allow people to discuss a certain issue or offer and then come to a conclusion during the meeting. In Japan, however, ad hoc decisions cannot be made since all members of a team (including those not present) need to be consulted. A Japanese meeting is an event in which partners come together, get to know each other, and develop a good relationship. Information exchange also plays a very important role in Japanese meetings, but in most cases, they are not meant to allow all participants to express their opinions and to come to a conclusion within a limited time frame.

Meetings in Japan have the following intentions:

- Allow as many members of each firm to meet and get to know each other
- Establish a friendly relationship with the partner firm
- Get information that has not yet been gathered
- Make sure all participants are on the same page

So when doing business in Japan, it is advisable to calculate a longer time frame than when doing business with European or American business partners. In most meetings, no decisions will be made. Japanese negotiators always have to go back to their company and discuss and decide issues with a wider range of people. In case there is a vote or final decision in a meeting, this decision has been agreed on beforehand and is only sanctioned at the meeting. One can only expect fast results when dealing with a company that has extensive experience negotiating with Western firms.

Meetings With Japanese Business Partners

Japanese companies and their employees place great importance on preparation. Every detail of a meeting or event is planned long beforehand. This also includes gathering information about a new business partner's company, all their products, and their business in other parts of the world. It is therefore not unusual to receive a list of very detailed questions before a negotiation, or even before a first meeting. Many of the questions may not seem related to the current business encounter at all.

These questions usually reoccur for quite some time and sometimes create anger and confusion on the Western side. Western companies are not accustomed to sharing information this freely.

The reason for this curiosity is the Japanese tendency to create long-term relationships in business and to avoid risk (by finding out as much as possible about the potential business partner). Japanese companies often fear that a foreign business partner will pull out of the Japanese market once problems occur or business is not going well. This could lead to problems for the Japanese firm, especially if they receive supply materials or special services from a foreign firm. To avoid any risks of unreliable business partners, they screen them very carefully and make sure they can build a long-lasting and future-oriented relationship.

It is very advisable to take care of the relationship in the Japanese way. Always ensure that you go to your first meeting well prepared. Asking questions about the firm, as the Japanese do, allows free flow of information and shows interest in your counterpart's firm.

Meeting Etiquette

Don't Be on Time: Be Early!

It is very important not to be late. The overall rule when meeting with a Japanese client is "Don't be on time, be early!" Being late is not excused in Japan. Having a Japanese business partner wait is considered extremely rude. It is common to show up a few minutes early. In case there is a delay (even 5 minutes!), it is advisable to call the office and apologize. Excuses such as "There was a lot of traffic" or "I did not find my way around" are not accepted in Japan. When Japanese people hear excuses like this they think, "There is always a lot of traffic, just leave the house earlier!"

Greetings and Gift Giving

The introduction is an important part of the first meeting. Usually, all participants are introduced according to their rank. This is also the time when presents are exchanged. Presents play an important part in Asian business culture and reflect the interest and sympathy of the giver. Japanese managers usually prefer food presents, particularly local food from the hometown or area in which the company is located. Gift giving is taken very seriously in Japan and serves as a means of establishing sound personal and business relationships. There are specific guidelines for types, prices, and packaging of gifts.[2] Business travelers in Japan need to consider two types of gifts: personal gifts, for those individuals who have gone out of their way to help them, and group gifts, for the entire group, section, or company they are visiting.[3] Due to the hierarchical structure of the Japanese society, brand, price, and packaging of presents must be in accordance with the status of both the giver and the recipient.[4]

Japanese business meetings start with a "warm up" in the form of small talk. Small talk usually circulates around very general issues such as the weather or where people are from. Family issues or relationships and political events are not discussed. The most important aspect at this point in the meeting is establishing a relaxed and friendly atmosphere between all participants of the meeting.

Exchanging Business Cards

Exchanging name cards or business cards is an important issue. These are mostly used to tell the recipient about the hierarchical status of the card giver. Since human interaction is strongly influenced by the position of the communicators, cards convey information that is more important than that embedded in e-mail addresses or telephone numbers. Cards should be handed to the recipient in a way that allows him or her to read them easily. Japanese partners expect that business cards are treated with respect and are left on the table during a meeting. When planning long-term business in Japan, it is also advisable to bring name cards in Japanese, which has a substantial impact in terms of impression management. The position of the name-card holder should be translated carefully into the Japanese equivalent to increase understanding on the Japanese side. Nonprofessional translations can confuse Japanese partners or ridicule the name-card giver right at the beginning of the negotiations. The following text explains how to correctly exchange business cards in Japan.

How to Exchange Business Cards in Japan

In a business context, *meishi* are exchanged when introducing one-self for the first time. *Meishi* are usually kept in a protector case to preserve them, as their fresh appearance must reflect that of the beholder. When presenting one's card to another party, it should be held at the top corners and shown so that the receiver may read the giver's information immediately and grab the card at the two bottom corners. The words *"choudai-itashimasu"* normally accompany the presentation of the card, at which point both parties bow to each other. If a person of lower standing exchanges cards with one of higher status, the subordinate is to bow longer and lower and should hand the card lower than that of the superior. Following the way the information is stated on one's card, company name, division or title, and name should be spoken in this order. If receiving a card, it should be carefully considered and handled gently, and information on the card should be immediately memorized and the giver's standing should be noted. Following the introductory conversation, the *meishi* should be gently laid on a table and kept in front of oneself or inserted at the back of a card filer if parting with the giver.

Certain gestures and attitudes surrounding the process of exchanging *meishi* are generally understood as insults. Some notorious examples are folding a card in two, placing the card in one's pocket, receiving the card with one hand, placing one's fingers over a name or other information on the card, not bowing when receiving the card, not reading the card when it is received, not remembering one's name and having to read it off the card afterward, writing on the card, and using the card to fan oneself or in any other playful manner.

Other behaviors, although they may not be regarded as direct insults, are to be avoided as they might be viewed as clumsy. For instance, presenting one's card with the name upside down (from the point of view of the receiver) or presenting the English side up to a Japanese speaker could be viewed as careless. Not placing the card in an orderly manner onto the table might also tickle the sensitivity of the person who gave it, as it would suggest that the receiver does think of the giver with respect.

As a rule of thumb, it is safe to remember that the *meishi* incarnates one's standing, achievements, pride, and identity. It is thus to be handled accordingly, with similar respect the person in question deserves, which implies sensitivity, attention to detail, and devotion.[5]

Recognizing the Most Influential Person

In a Japanese meeting, it is often a bit difficult to decipher who is in charge and has the highest rank. During the meeting, all participants are seated according to their rank. Japanese *kaigi* (meetings) *are* very strict in regard to the traditional rule of seating arraignments. The highest-ranked person usually sits the farthest from the rear (this is called *kamiza*) and the lowest-ranked person sits nearest to the door (*shimoza*). The most influential Japanese person often does not speak English well enough to lead the conversation, and younger managers will speak instead of him. This, however, does not mean that they have any decision-making power or can influence the Japanese group discussion that usually takes place after the meeting. Japanese people are expected to know the seating arrangement, and the traditional Japanese seating arrangement is also reflected in daily social happenings such as dinner, drinking events, and *kaigi* between two different companies. Non-Japanese business people should, in any case, ask where to be seated. Rushing into a restaurant and taking the seat next to the window is not a very good idea.

Size and Time

Japanese prefer large negotiation teams because they require wider participation within their corporations to make decisions.[6] Hence, meetings mostly start with the exchange of non-task-related information and a brief introduction of all participants. Most negotiations are conducted by middle managers. Since the Japanese are very rank conscious, their Western counterparts should not be officers of lower rank because this may imply a lack of seriousness in the undertaking. Furthermore, as in most

Asian countries, age is synonymous with wisdom and experience. It may be advisable to meet Japanese business partners with colleagues of older age, even if they are not allowed to make decisions. During the negotiations, it is very important to distinguish and address the senior decision makers on the Japanese side. In many cases, they will be the oldest members of the team and they may not speak English. Younger members of a Japanese negotiation team are very likely to speak better English, but they will have little influence.[7]

Circular Discussion Style

In terms of time, a *kaigi* is very slow and often takes 3 times as long as a Western meeting. Since the Japanese do not come to a conclusion unless everyone agrees, it takes much longer to come to a decision. Japanese culture does not tolerate the majority rule but tries to include everyone's ideas and come to a mutual decision where everyone is happy and respected. From an American perspective, it could be annoyingly slow; however, culturally, Japanese people are accustomed to doing things in a way that values groupism and keeps the harmony (*wa*).

Concerning negotiations and information-gathering behavior, Japanese prefer a more circular style. Every aspect of the topic needs to be discussed, sometimes even two or more times. Factors that are not related to the topic in Western eyes may be of great interest to the Japanese. Meetings in Japan therefore usually take much longer than in the West. Decisions are not usually made during a business meeting. Western negotiators should therefore not expect to come up with a contract or a sales order by the end of a first business meeting but should try to make their point clear and give the Japanese the possibility of finding a suitable solution after the meeting. If possible, problems or unexpected events should be solved beforehand in a process called *nemawashi* (see chapter 6).

After the Meeting

Going out after work is customary for Japanese business people and usually also obligatory for foreign partners. These events are usually carefully organized dinners in restaurants. Business dinners usually last about 2 or 3 hours and may start as early as 6:30 p.m. They offer a good networking opportunity because they establish more personal relationships between all the participants. They also serve the function of relaxing all the members of a company and allowing informal communication with superiors or customers.

Summary

- The concept of the business meeting generally conveys different meanings in Japanese and Western cultures. The main purpose of the Japanese business meeting is to meet and inform participants and to create some common understanding about the topic at hand. Meetings are therefore often used to gain as much information as possible from Western counterparts, and traditionally, they are used to exchange information and to build stronger relationships between all participants. In Table 9.1, we can see a summary of the dos and don'ts when negotiating with the Japanese.

- Japanese negotiators always attempt to develop a good relationship with all participants of a meeting or negotiation. It is advisable to take time to build a friendly and relaxed relationship with Japanese business partners. Japanese meeting culture is very particular. Japanese negotiation meetings tend to be large and are often led by an older manager who does not speak English. In the meeting, seating arrangements are prearranged. The most influential person seats near the window or the farthest from the door; the younger participants are seated next to the entrance of the meeting room.

- Cold calls were once typically avoided in contacting potential Japanese partners. In past years, however, the recession and internationalization of Japanese business has changed this unspoken rule a bit, and polite cold calls have proven to be very successful for many foreign investors. At the first meeting with a potential client, it is recommended that a Japanese employee attend the meeting with you to signal that your company respects "the Japanese way."

- During the meeting, discussion is circular and may touch the same topic more than once. Open conflict or a direct confrontation should be avoided. The meeting often ends with dinner or another social function.

Table 9.1. Dos and Don'ts When Negotiating With the Japanese[8]

Dos
• Be patient.
• Collect as much information as possible before the meeting.
• Be 10 to 15 minutes early.
• Bring name cards in Japanese (translated by a professional translator).
• Bring an interpreter to make sure you get all the details.
• Create a friendly and relaxed atmosphere.
• Always address the person of highest rank with the appropriate respect.
• Bring presents typical for your home town (such as food specialties).
• Bring written information to every meeting with your Japanese business partners.
• Accept all invitations for informal dinners or meetings.
• After the meeting, give Japanese partners time to reflect on the offers.
• Be even more patient!
Don'ts
• Avoid physical contact, like hugging and clapping someone's shoulder.
• Don't get impatient when negotiations are taking a great deal longer than expected.
• Don't eat in public places or while walking in the street.
• Avoid being cynical or ironic.
• Don't discuss politics or personal problems with Japanese business partners.
• Don't openly contradict business partners.
• Don't get irritated when Japanese business partners are silent for minute or two.

PART III

What Can Western Managers Learn From Japan?

CHAPTER 10

Learning From Japanese Management

In the 1980s, Japanese management seemed to be the more advanced way of organizing a firm and taking care of human resources. At that time, production management had the greatest influence on Western corporations simply because Japanese manufacturers spent less time and money producing their products. Just-in-time and total quality management were copied by Western firms and implemented very successfully. Other traditional Japanese management practices, such as human resource management and knowledge management, were not as successfully exported. The reasons for this are obvious: These styles are strongly related to Japanese group-oriented values and cannot be easily implemented in a Western corporation, where individualism dominates.

But Japanese management has moved beyond developing effective manufacturing processes and lifetime employment. Not only were traditional Japanese management practices strongly affected by social changes in Japan over the past decades, but Japanese firms were also massively restructured during the recession of the 1990s. Because of all these changes, what we can learn from Japanese management practices has changed, too. The global financial crisis of the past years leaves us with doubts concerning whether Western management styles are as efficient and as human and future oriented as we thought. With all the economic issues and turnover in Western companies, many people are clamoring for different ideas regarding how successful enterprises are run. The economic crisis and the discussion of how management styles have created it are leading to a search for new approaches to business management. Western management models no longer offer answers regarding how to provide security and wealth. Again, the West is looking for new ideas. Fresh perspectives are being considered, and the question of whether

Japanese companies and management styles can again provide inspirations and alternative ideas is becoming relevant again. Following the "lost decade," the Japanese have learned hard lessons and have developed management processes and ideas that can inspire managers in other cultures.[1] Now that trust in traditional Western management processes is vanishing, Japanese approaches may provide answers concerning how to create long-lasting business success. These answers may not involve practical advice, such as how to improve a manufacturing process, but may be more philosophical, allowing Western managers to benefit from Japanese values and attitudes toward business.

The following sections will review several aspects of modern Japanese management that are worth investigating and learning from.

Stability Focus

One aspect that is particularly interesting about Japanese management is the long-term perspective of Japanese corporations. Business in Japan is not about making a single profitable deal; instead, it is about building long, and often lifelong, relationships with business partners, customers, and employees. Money is important but not the most important aspect of managing a Japanese firm. Japanese companies have stability in mind—stability not only for themselves but also for all of their stakeholders. This attitude was viewed as one of the major problems during the Japanese recession, where Japanese companies tried to keep their employees, as they found it very difficult to cut unprofitable, but traditional, relationships with expensive suppliers or distributors.

Today, the long-term and people-oriented attitude of Japanese firms is no longer considered naïve or unrealistic. Japanese companies managed to shape up their firms during the 1990s without dramatic layoffs and social uproar, a task many Western firms will face both now and in the future. Here, the Japanese experience can be of great value. In this area, Japanese corporations can again be role models for Western firms.

Motivation and Dedication to Work

The atmosphere in a Japanese firm is usually very friendly. Many employees still enjoy lifetime employment; they do not fear losing their jobs;

they get paid according to their time in the firm (seniority system); and competition inside the firm is very low. For many Western managers, this seems quite odd, and they wonder how people can be motivated if there is no individual appraisal and achievement-based gratification.

The answer for Western management is simple. A relaxed and less stressful atmosphere allows all members to dedicate themselves to their tasks. Motivation is improved by working in a group and by feeling an emotional connection to it. Strong, group-oriented motivation can be found when Western managers work in a Japanese group. This group cohesion leads to a lower number of micropolitical problems than in Western business. To improve cooperation and dedication to work, Japanese companies employ various tools that help to increase the cooperation among employees. These Japanese group motivation and team-building techniques may also provide some inspiration for non-Japanese businesses.

New Product Development

New product development techniques in Japan may not lead to radical innovations all the time, but these techniques have supported Japanese firms in sustaining their competitive advantage as customer-oriented manufacturers. The ways in which new and small ideas are discussed in a circular form within a Japanese team allow corporations to integrate consumer ideas from the start of product development. Even if Western firms are more interested in radical innovation and change, small changes and product improvement can also lead to higher profits and business success.

Market and Consumer Orientation

Another strength of Japanese firms is their strong orientation toward clients and consumers. Japan, and especially Tokyo, is the most competitive business hub in the world. Companies trying to sell their products need to be heard, and they develop increasingly innovative approaches to address their consumers. On top of this, the Japanese market reflects many trends that are also developing in other industrialized countries, such as the increasing number of older and single consumers. Most markets have moved from price competition to quality competition, and Japanese service lessons often provide a base for improvements of multinational corporations. In Japan, this change in attitude is more obvious than in many other markets. Japanese consumers are expecting the world's best service, and Japanese firms have successfully adapted to these wishes. This type of attitude provides learning opportunities for Western corporations. Foreign enterprises in Japan usually have to change their service processes, too, if they wish to be successful in the Japanese market. Most non-Japanese corporations in Japan undergo a learning process and manage to improve their standards in the Japanese markets. Japan becomes a benchmark for many multinational corporations.

Involving Japanese consumers in product design and development, adapting products to their tastes, and allowing them to get in contact with one another are marketing strategies that could be successfully adopted in the West.

Learning From the Japanese

After many years of working in Japan, I have come to the conclusion that both management systems—the Japanese and the Western systems—have strengths and weaknesses. Both are very different from each other and both leave very much room to learn. When learning from the Japanese, however, one should not make the mistake of assuming Japanese management practices are characterized by one overall technique. Japanese management practices are actually very diverse, and in almost all business fields, Japanese businesses have developed different—and often inspiring—management processes.

Another of the major advantages of the Japanese business system is the fact that Japanese corporations and managers make judgments regarding new ideas or changes at a later stage in the process. They look at innovations and Western ideas from all angles, discuss them with their peers, and then pick the parts they find most interesting and promising. After this, the idea or product is "Japanized," which means it is improved and adapted to suit the Japanese customer or Japanese corporate needs. This practice, which is another reason for Japanese business success, is called *iitoko dori*. Iitoko dori is the Japanese term for picking the best of everything—looking at a new idea or product with open-minded curiosity and choosing the aspects that seem interesting and profitable and disregarding the ones that are not useful. In Japanese management practices, iitoko dori could be described as the process of adopting foreign imports and incorporating the best elements into their culture and their product portfolio, but not without adapting them to local tastes.

As non-Japanese managers, we should use iitoko dori to accomplish the same thing when learning about Japanese management practices and look at Japanese management practices as a set of new and inspiring tools that can be used independently from each other. Iitoko dori means to focus on useful details that can be used to solve problems in Western firms and to improve business processes and inspire employees. Some Japanese management practices may work well in a small family business but cannot be implemented in multinational corporations. Kaizen methods may be successfully implemented in a firm, but other Japanese management practices may not be accepted by non-Japanese employees. The overall idea of iitoko dori is that looking at the big picture (in our case, Japanese management as a whole) is sometimes less productive than focusing on details (such as specific Japanese management ideas and thoughts), which can provide useful inspirations and lead to business success when implemented (copied) in a new setting or environment. In this sense, Japanese management practices can provide a great inspiration for managers and corporations all over the world.

Glossary

andon. Light above a production line indicating whether there is a problem

ba. Place

bunkatsu hôshiki. Divided production system

burando ryoku. Brand power

bushido. The way of the samurai

freeter. Job-hopping part-time worker

gai(koku)jin. Foreigner

ganbaru. Do one's best

haken. Dispatch worker

hanseikai. Reflection meeting

hikikomori. Social dropout who constantly stays at home

hitori hôshiki. One-man production system

ippanshoku. Career in administration of a Japanese company

jidôka. Automation

jinmyaku. Personal relationships

junkai hôshiki. Chase production system

kaisha. Japanese firm

kaizen. Improvement

kanban. Card (used in manufacturing)

keiretsu. Japanese conglomerate

kôhai. One's junior (somebody who entered the company at a later stage)

manga. Comic book

naitei. Letter of acceptance; acceptance notice

NEET. Young person not in education, employment, or training

nomikai. Drinking party

otaku. Enthusiastic fan and consumer

salarymen. Office workers

seiketsu. Systematize

seiri. Sort

seishain. Regular employees

seiso. Clean

seiton. Setting in order

sekuhara. Sexual harassment (abbr.)

senpai. One's senior (somebody who entered the company at an earlier stage)

shain ryokô. Company outing

shinhatsubai. New release; new on sale

shinkaishahô. New company law

shinshôhin. New product

shitsuke. Standardize

sôgô shosha. General trading company

sôgôshoku. Career track in a Japanese company (nonadministrative work)

taishokukin. Allowance for retirement

tenshoku. Job change

tenshokusha. One who has changed jobs

wakon yôsai. Western talent with Japanese spirit

yokonarabi. Going along with the crowd

zaibatsu. Financial conglomerate

Notes

Chapter 1

1. Haghirian (2009a).
2. Imai (1986).

Chapter 2

1. Parry (2006).
2. Nomura Research Institute (2004).

Chapter 3

1. Hayakama et al. (2009).
2. Hayakama et al. (2009).

Chapter 4

1. Nonaka et al (2000).
2. Doz and Santos (1997).
3. Nonaka et al. (2001).
4. Doz and Santos (1997).
5. Nonaka et al. (2001); Nonaka (1994).
6. Polanyi (1969).
7. Hentschel and Haghirian (2010).
8. Hentschel and Haghirian (2010).
9. Nonaka et al. (2000).
10. Nonaka (1994).
11. Haghirian (2010).
12. Nonaka et al. (2001).
13. Nonaka (1994).
14. Nonaka (1994).
15. Nonaka et al. (2001).
16. Nonaka (1994).

17. Nonaka (1994).
18. Nonaka (2001).
19. Nonaka (1994).
20. Nonaka (2001).
21. Nonaka and Takeuchi (1995).
22. Clarry (2010).
23. Clarry (2010).
24. Hentschel and Haghirian (2011).
25. Hentschel and Haghirian (2010).
26. Hentschel and Haghirian (2010).

Chapter 5

1. Fields et al. (2000).
2. Roland Berger (2005).
3. Zaheer (1995).
4. Haghirian (2006).
5. Roland Berger (2005).
6. Roland Berger (2005).
7. Haghirian (2006).
8. Haghirian et al. (2008).
9. Haghirian (2006).
10. Haghirian (2006).
11. Abbeglen and Stalk (1996).
12. Haghirian (2009b).
13. Fields, et al. (2000).
14. Gaspari (2010).

Chapter 6

1. Melville (1999).
2. De Mente (1994).
3. Hall and Hall (1987).
4. Hall and Hall (1987).
5. Dunung (1998).
6. Dunung (1998).
7. Kondansha (2003).
8. Shinomiya and Szepkouski (2002).
9. Based on Neuman (2009).

Chapter 7

1. Befu (2001).
2. United Nations (2008).
3. Sugimoto (2003), p. 157.
4. Japanese Ministry of Health, Labor and Welfare (2008).
5. Haghirian (2009b).

Chapter 8

1. Haghirian and Gaspari (2009).
2. Schuette and Ciarlante (1998).
3. Solomon et al. (1999).
4. Schuette and Ciarlante (1998).
5. Maamria (2001).
6. Schneidewind (1998).
7. Schuette and Ciarliante (1998); Schneidewind (1998).
8. Schuette and Ciarlante (1998).
9. Sanga and Nishida (2009).
10. Lasserre and Schuette (1999).
11. Schuette and Ciarlante (1998).
12. Samiee and Mayo (1990).
13. Skov and Moeran (1995).
14. Kohlbacher and Haghirian (2007).
15. McCreery (2000).
16. Schuette and Ciarliante (1998); Solomon et al. (1999); Skov and Moeran (1995).
17. McCreery (2000).
18. Agulhon and Haghirian (2010).
19. Kitabashi (2005).
20. Usunier (2000).
21. Schuette and Ciarlante (1998).
22. Morgan and Morgan (1991).
23. Melville (1999).
24. Schuette and Ciarliante (1998).
25. Schuette and Ciarlante (1998).
26. Schuette and Ciarlante (1998).
27. Melville (1999); Schneidewind (1998).
28. Maamria (2001).
29. Schuette and Ciarlante (1998).

Chapter 9

1. El Kahal (2001).
2. Dunung (1998).
3. Brannen (2003).
4. Lasserre and Schuette (1999).
5. Gagnon (2010).
6. Chen (2004).
7. Dunung (1998).
8. Adapted from Haghirian et al. 2008.

Chapter 10

1. Haghirian (2009d).

References

Abbeglen, J. C., & Stalk, G. J. (1996). *Kaisha, the Japanese corporation*. Tokyo: Charles E. Tuttle.

Agulhon, V., & Haghirian, P. (2010). *Sony Playstation 3: Phoenix from the flames? Marketing strategy in the Japanese video market*. Case study submitted to the European Case Clearing House. Retrieved from http://www.ecch.cranfield.ac.uk

Befu, H. (2001). *Hegemony of homogeneity: An anthropological analysis of Nihonjinron*. North Victoria, Australia: Trans Pacific Press.

Brannen, C. (2003). *Going to Japan on business; Protocol, strategies, and language for the corporate traveller*. Berkeley, CA: Stone Bridge Press.

Chen, M. (2004). *Asian management systems*. London: Thompson.

Clarry, J. (2010). Innovation and the patenting of knowledge in Japanese corporations. In P. Haghirian (Ed.), *Innovation and change in Japanese management* (pp. 177–198). London: Palgrave Macmillan.

De Mente, B. (1994). *Japanese etiquette & ethics in business*. Chicago: NTC Business Books.

Dunung, S. P. (1998). *Doing business in Asia: The complete guide*. San Francisco: Jossey-Bass.

Doz, Y., & Santos, J. (1997). *On the management of knowledge: From the transparency of colocation and co-setting to the quandary of dispersion and differentiation*. Fontainebleau, France: INSEAD Working Paper.

El Kahal, S. (2001). *Business in Asia-Pacific: Text and cases*. Oxford: Oxford University Press.

Fields, G., Katahira, H., & Wind, J. (2000). *Leveraging Japan: Marketing for the new Asia*. San Francisco: Jossey-Bass.

Gagnon, P. (2010). Unpublished working paper, Sophia University, Tokyo, Japan: Gakken.

Gakken. (2002). Japan as it is. Tokyo: Gakken.

Gaspari, P. (2010). Entering the Japanese market: The important rules you should know first. Retrieved from http://www.paulgaspari.com

Haghirian, P., R. Sinkovics, and V. Bamiatzi. (2008, November/December). Japan: New business opportunities in an established market. *Global Business and Organizational Excellence*, pp. 51–61.

Haghirian, P. (2006, July). Erfolgreiche Marktbearbeitung in Japan–Herausforderung für europäische Unternehmen. *Japan Markt*.

Haghirian, P. (2009a). Kaizen. In C. Wankel (Ed.), *Encyclopedia of business in today's world*. Thousand Oaks, CA: Sage.

Haghirian, P. (2009b, August). Opportunities for international women in Japan. *Being A Broad Magazine*, p. 19.

Haghirian, P. (2009c, August). Do's and don'ts im japanischen marketing (Do's and don'ts in Japanese marketing). Japan Markt, pp. 6–8.

Haghirian, P. (2009d, July/August). Japanese management after the lost decade: Can we learn from Japan again? The revival of Japanese management. *Japan Spotlight*, pp. 36–37.

Haghirian, P. (2010). Multinationals and cross-cultural management: The transfer of knowledge within multinational corporations. London: Routledge.

Haghirian, P., & Gaspari, P. (2009, December). Evolution: Consumer marketing goes 2.0 in Tokyo as the customers take control. *ACCJ Journal*. Tokyo: American Chamber of Commerce. Retrieved from http://accjjournal.com/evolution/

Hall, E. T., & Hall, M. R. (1987). *Hidden differences, doing business with the Japanese*. New York: Anchor Books, Doubleday.

Hayakama, N., Okachi, M., & Kalbermatten, P. (2009). Production management. In P. Haghirian (Ed.), *Japanese management: Fresh perspectives on the Japanese firm in the 21st century* (pp. 147–179). Bloomington, IN: iUniverse.

Hentschel, B., & Haghirian, P. (2010). Nonaka revisited: Can Japanese companies sustain their knowledge management processes in the 21st century? In P. Haghirian (Ed.), *Innovation and change in Japanese management* (pp. 199–220). London: Palgrave Macmillan.

Hentschel, B., & Haghirian, P. (2011). *Social knowledge in Japan*. In J. Girard (Ed.), *Social knowledge: Using social media to know what you know*. Idea Group Publishing (forthcoming).

Imai, M. (1986). *Kaizen: The key to Japan's competitive success*. New York, NY: McGraw-Hill/Irwin

Japanese Ministry of Health, Labor and Welfare (2008). *White paper on gender equality*. Retrieved from http://www.gender.go.jp/whitepaper/ewp2008.pdf

Jetro. (2003). 2003 Jetro White Paper on International Trade and Foreign Direct Investment.

Jetro. (2004). *Nippon: Business facts and figures*. Tokyo: Japan External Trade Organization.

Kitabashi, K. (2005). The otaku group from a business perspective: Revaluation of enthusiastic consumers. Nomura Research Report No. 84, December 1, 2004. Retrieved from http://www. nri.co.jp/

Kohlbacher, F., & Haghirian, P. (2007, January). Japan und das Wissen der Babyboomer [Japan and the babyboomers' knowledge]. Wissensmanagement, pp. 22–24.

Kondansha. (2003). *Bairingaru Nihon Jiten.* Tokyo: Kodansha International.

Kriska, L. (1998). *The accidental office lady.* Tokyo: Tuttle Publishing.

Lasserre, P., & Schuette, H. (1999). *Strategies of Asia Pacific: Beyond the crisis,* London: Palgrave Macmillan.

Maamria, K. (2001). Made in Japan. *Telecommunications* (International Edition), *35*(2), 90–94.

McCreery, J. (2000). *Japanese consumer behavior: From worker bees to wary shoppers.* London: RoutledgeCurzon.

Melville, I. (1999). *Marketing in Japan.* Oxford: Butterworth-Heinemann.

Morgan, J. C., & Morgan, J. J. (1991). *Cracking the Japanese market: Strategies for success in the new global economy.* New York: Free Press.

Neuman, A. (2009). *Managing Japan-U.S. project teams: Keys for intercultural success.* Presentation at the 2nd Japan Intercultural Institute Conference, Shirayuri College, Tokyo.

Nomura Research Institute, Ltd. (2004, November 1). *Over 90% of people have a sense of crisis regarding the NEET issue.* Retrieved from http://www.nri.co.jp/english/news/2004/041101.html

Nonaka, I. (1994). A dynamic theory of organizational knowledge creation. *Organization Science, 5*(1), 14–37.

Nonaka, I., & Takeuchi, H. (1995). *The knowledge creating company: How Japanese companies create the dynamics of innovation.* New York: Oxford University Press.

Nonaka, I., Reinmoeller, P., & Senoo, D. (2000). Integrated IT systems to capitalize on market knowledge. In G. von Krogh (Ed.), *Knowledge creation: A source of value* (pp. 89–109). London: Palgrave Macmillan.

Nonaka, I., Toyama, R., & Konno, N. (2001). SECI, *ba* and leadership: A unified model of dynamic knowledge creation. In I. Nonaka (Ed.), *Managing industrial knowledge: Creation, transfer and utilization* (pp. 13–43). London: Sage.

Parry, R. L. (2006, November 2). *A nation lives in a fear of the Neets and Freeters. Times Online.* Retrieved from http://business.timesonline.co.uk/tol/business/markets/japan/article622158.ece

Polanyi, M. (1969). *The tacit dimension.* New York: Doubleday. Roland Berger. (2005). *Making money in Japan: A profitability survey among German affili¬ates in Japan.* Tokyo: Roland Berger Strategy Consultants & Deutsche Industrie- und Handelskammer in Japan.

Samiee, S., & Mayo, A. (1990). Barriers to trade with Japan: A socio-cultural perspective. *European Journal of Marketing, 24*(12), 48–66.

Sanga, A. & Nishida, J. (2009). Marketing. In P. Haghirian (Ed.), *J-Management; Fresh perspectives on the Japanese firm in the 21st century* (pp. 180–203). Bloomington: iUniverse Star.

Schneidewind, D. (1998). Shinhatsubai. München: Beck.

Schuette, H., & Ciarlante, D. (1998). *Consumer behavior in Asia*. London: Macmillan.

Shinomiya, S., & Szepkouski, B. (2002). *Business passport to Japan*. Tokyo: ICG Muse.

Skov, L., & Moeran, B. (1995). *Women, media and consumption in Japan*. Honolulu: University of Hawai'i Press.

Solomon, M., Bamossy, G., & Askegaard, S. (1999). *Consumer behaviour: A European perspective*. New York: Prentice Hall Europe.

Sugimoto, Y. (2003). *An introduction to Japanese society*. Cambridge: Cambridge University Press.

United Nations. (2008). *Gender empowerment measure*. Retrieved from http://www.hdr.undp.org/en/media/HDR_20072008_GEM.pdf

Usunier, J.-C. (2000). *Marketing across cultures*. Harlow, NJ: Pearson Education Limited.

Zaheer, S. (1995). Overcoming the liability of foreignness. *Academy of Management Journal, 38*(2), 341–361.

Index

Note: Page numbers followed by a "t" indicate tables.

E
education, 16–17, 24
endurance, 15, 79–80
entrepreneurs, 70–74
explicit knowledge, 39–40, 42–43
externalization conversions, 42–43

F
failure, 86
5S System, 3, 7–8, 8t
freeters, 24
full-time employment, 14, 16
fuyuso (new rich), 111–12

G
gaijin (non-Japanese) companies, 56,
    119, 123, 127
gaman (endurance), 15, 79–80
ganbaru (perseverance), 15, 79, 86
Gaspari, Paul, 58
Gates, Bill, 47
gemba (actual workplace) *kaizen*, 5.
    See also 5S System
genchi genbutsu (go and see for your-
    self), 10–11
gender issues, 103. *See also* women
generalists, 22, 26, 28
gentei (limited edition), 109–10, 122
gifts, 129–30
goals, 85
go and see for yourself, 10–11
groupism, 92–95. *See also* group
    structures
group structures
    change and, 5–6
    human resource management and,
        3, 9–12, 18–20, 25–26, 140
    intercultural challenges and, 92–95,
        100, 105
    knowledge management and,
        45–46
    marketing and, 114, 119–20
    senior-junior system and, 14–15,
        18–19, 28, 29, 100–101

H
haichi tenkan (job rotation), 11,
    28–29

hakensha (contracted workers), 24
Hall, E. T., 76
Hall, M. R., 76
hanseikai (reflection meetings), 11–12
heijunka (production leveling),
    33–34, 37
hierarchical structure, 44
high-context communication, 76–77
hitori hôshiki (one-man production
    system), 37
hobbyists, 113–14
honne (private) opinions, 77–78, 88
honorific language, 76, 88
Howl of the Loser Dog, The (Sakai),
    113
human resource management
    entering a Japanese organization
        and, 15–17
    group orientation and, 3, 14–15
    group structure and, 18–20, 25–26
    lifetime employment and, 20–23
    NEETS and, 25
    overview, 13
    part-time employment and, 24
    summary, 29–30
    trade unions and, 26–27
    training and, 27–29

I
iitoko dori (Japanization), 85, 142–43
Imai, Masaaki, 4
indirectness, 96–97
industrialization of Japan, 21
infrastructure, 57
inside-outside, 14, 15–17
intercultural challenges
    foreign women and, 101–4
    groupism and, 92–95
    indirectness and, 96–97
    language and, 91–92
    overview, 91
    private and professional time con-
        flicts as, 97–99
    relationships and, 100–101
    summary, 105–6
internalization conversions, 42, 43
INVEST Japan, 56
investments, 56–58